A DECLARATION OF
AMERICAN BUSINESS VALUES
★★★

Published by:
Values of America Company
Cherry Hill, New Jersey
Phone: 866-467-7304
E-mail: orders@americanbusinessvalues.com
Web: www.americanbusinessvalues.com

Cover Design by Marybeth Polischak/ AlphaGraphics
Cover Photograph by Tom Brakefield/ Getty Images

ISBN-13   978-0-9765868-1-4
ISBN-10   0-9765868-1-9

Library of Congress Control Number: 2006934317

Printed in the United States of America

A DECLARATION OF AMERICAN BUSINESS VALUES
★★★

ETHICS, EQUITY and EFFICIENCY in the NEW MILLENNIUM

Robert L. Merz

2006

A DECLARATION OF
AMERICAN BUSINESS VALUES
★★★

ACKNOWLEDGMENTS
★★★

Looking at the business organization as a family is the easiest way to put together a progressive game plan. Wherein each member of a family has a role, so does each individual within the company. The key point is a mutual respect and understanding between members. The managers and future leaders of American business must realize the link between the home life of employees and climate of the work culture. Taking a keen interest in the individual, and merging the goals of each party, will go a long way in defining the functional family.

With this portrait in place, I would like to thank the following families for showing me what it takes to get the job done—and do it well. Firstly, The Merz Group (not to be confused with by brother Andy's award-winning advertising agency) has given me the independence and support necessary to achieve. The Broussards have always been there with words of wisdom and worldly perspectives. The Gross Family has defined the word brotherhood in Philadelphia, shining a bright light. The Goldenbergs have taught me what it takes to be successful in business—one based on family values and creativity. The Forests have given me a clear appreciation of how a diverse group of personalities creates a positive force. From the Harris and Paul families, I have seen the innovative spirit and concern for others passed down to the new generations. Also, to Dave Ludlum, Jim Myers, and Robert Rosen for showing me that it takes perseverance and hard work to excel.

Finally, to the faculty and staff who provided insights and encouragements, in particular, Dr. Harold Hawkins of The University of Oregon, and Dr. Thomas Ktsanes of Tulane University.

About the Author
★★★

Robert L. Merz is a native Philadelphian, who grew up in the shadows of Independence Hall and the Liberty Bell, with an appreciation for American history.

He holds a Master's degree in Industrial Relations from the University of Oregon, and a Bachelor's degree in Sociology from Tulane University. He has worked for several Fortune 500 companies in the fields of sales, marketing, and management. He has participated in several structured, corporate management-training programs, and been involved in an entrepreneurial start-up business. He currently resides in Cherry Hill, New Jersey.

The ideas presented in this book are the culmination of research that began over three decades ago—developing from a scholastic history paper on The Coca-Cola Company; to a university independent study project highlighting the sociological value systems of companies; to post graduate study and consulting work in organization development; to practical work experience covering varying aspects of business management.

TABLE OF CONTENTS

to Leon Merz Jr.
who sparked this idea
35 years ago

What we must decide is how we are valuable, rather than how valuable we are.

F. Scott Fitzgerald

PREFACE
★★★

Given the renewed interest in American patriotism and the re-examination of our ideals, *A Declaration of American Business Values* serves as a treatise or affirmation of our historical values. This study is a guide to exploring the cultural value systems of America, and their applications to business organizations. At times, looking inward can bring solutions to societal, individual, and organizational challenges.

The book's principles are simple. Although we have access to the highest degree of technical knowledge, it is human relations and the defining of our cultural values that will be the guiding lights in the new millennium. As an applied science, this composition is not an attempt to favor secularism or stray from the religious convictions necessary to lead a spiritual life. Furthermore, the principles outlined are not an endorsement for a national "industrial democracy" similar to those of Western Europe. The United States is a unique country with a special heritage, representing the "collective individualism" of diverse viewpoints.

Incorporating ideas from the preeminent American social scientists of the twentieth century, this work aims to attract readers wanting to learn more about history, commerce, and culture. The subject matter has roots in the fields of sociology, psychology, philosophy, and business management.

Rather than a blueprint for the effective company, the value systems discussed serve as a conceptual framework for achieving excellence in the business world. Improving productivity and efficiency are goals of all organizations. Solving problems, increasing sales, motivating employees, and producing quality, are performance factors based on understanding the interrelationship of many variables.

A *Declaration of American Business Values* stresses a qualitative approach. It steers away from acting as a strictly quantitative barometer of technical solutions and plug-in management techniques. What follows are guidelines and ideas fundamental to American culture that are applicable to all entities. A so-called "Contract for American Business" is the intention of the book—relevant to companies of any size, domain, structure, or sector.

PART I

DEFINING & DESIGNING
AMERICAN BUSINESS VALUES
★★★

*Each of us brings to our job, whatever it is,
our lifetime of experience and our values.*

Sandra Day O'Connor

Chapter One

INTRODUCTION TO AMERICAN VALUES
★★★

This writing is an examination of American culture. What are the values that dictate life in America and where did they come from? More important, how can we take this value system and constructively apply it to the twenty-first-century business community? Values are vital because they motivate the behavior of a people and give a culture its distinctive quality.

Sociologists often refer to culture as the social heritage of a society. It is a mosaic of customs, beliefs, and behaviors giving a human community its characteristic flavor. In the field of applied psychology, the work culture is a place where individual, organizational, and societal needs merge. From a philosophical point of view, the workplace provides meaningful life experiences, and helps define the individual's role in society. In addition, business organizations represent open systems, subject to turbulence and ethical dilemmas.

What are the qualities that define American business culture? The American emphasis on success has stemmed from several sources—the Puritan Ethic of the colonial period; the frontier spirit that dominated westward population movement; and the capitalistic ethic underlying our industrial social order.

American business has given us the highest standard of living in the world. It is essential to understand how a system of free enterprise works. How from small beginnings, with creative ideas and industry, we have been able to build business institutions, making our nation strong at home and abroad.

A Declaration of American Business Values highlights the core value systems of American culture. These are: *Individualism and Progress; Equality and Equity; Ethics and Morality; Work and Achievement; Productivity and Efficiency;* and *Unity and Patriotism.*

The innovative and progressive organization implements all these value systems, forming a complete, workable model. This complex process takes time and requires acceptance by all participants. The organization aspiring to achieve these goals finds itself prepared for future change, and positioned to maximize productivity.

From an American business generalist point of view, acquiring material goods, striving for economic independence, and attaining symbols of prestige are goals held in high esteem. Any individual, regardless of background or ascribed status, having the dedication and devotion to get involved to the best of one's ability, can succeed.

Americans place considerable attention on making money. The idea is to always have an open mind, look for new opportunities, and strengthen the position already established. Production of goods is the foundation of economic health. The acceleration toward increasingly efficient production is an important denominator of the American economy.

When looking at the entire sphere of organizations— including not-for-profit, educational institutions, medical facilities, and charitable foundations, the value component takes center stage. Although the profit motive may take a back seat to creating an effective operation, it is still crucial to keep a close eye on productivity.

Regarding the unionized sector of commerce, the collective-bargaining mechanism often deals with quality of work issues alongside usual wage and benefit contracts. The historical evolution of unions in America can be traced to demands for better working conditions and fair treatment.

When unions in the twenty-first century draw up contracts with value-laden incentives, their strength grows as management-labor goals merge.

Traditionally, the central value in economic life has been individualism. The belief is that everything rests on giving each individual the latitude to achieve fulfillment. Complimentary to this principle are the affiliated ideas of competition, freedom, success, and equal opportunity.

The Early image of American society paints a picture of individuals having the freedom to go their own way, and find a comfort level contingent on their effort and performance. There was a striving to master one's environment, where work and progress played major roles. Making a living was a way of life, intertwined with an interest in community welfare.

The American value of freedom specifies that everyone has the same opportunity and choice. Looking at this doctrine and intending to help others, is the core of a real equality. The true way to bring groups or individuals together is through concerned people. This means helping for the sake of not only material wealth, but also growth and compassion. Humanitarianism and philanthropy are moral obligations centered on improving the human condition.

Americans tend to see the world in moral terms. This vision is not mere conformity to a particular moral code, but to a systematic moral orientation that judges conduct. Thinking in terms of right or wrong, ethical or unethical, reflect this normative structure. America was founded on the religious ethos of its citizens, that called for leading an orderly life, having a name for integrity, and favoring fair dealing.

In every society, people participate in groups to which they feel loyalty and a certain affinity. Within these groups, individuals can identify and define themselves. America has gained the loyalty of its people because it represents certain values that are prime objects of allegiance.

In the new millennium, American business will be reaching a crossroads and looking for answers. America's commercial mind power has brought us from a merchant class, agrarian village lifestyle; through a booming industrial society; and into a technologically advanced world. The twentieth century cultivated many revolutionary inventions and brought forth a staggering level of innovation. As technology moves forward, the keys to stabilizing and advancing the work culture rest in our understanding each other as individual and group. The human resource element becomes the dominant factor. Issues such as pay equity, corporate social responsibility, and the role of the individual, rise to the top.

Freedom in America
★★★

The history of freedom in America can be traced to liberties of the late Middle Ages, where trade and commerce grew out of a new merchant and artisan class. Communities were formed seeking independence and self-government from feudal barons.

The original thirteen American colonies saw freedom as a way of life in conducting their business and personal matters. Freedom was a means of standing up to overpowering leaders who exercised undue influence against the people's will. To the colonists, this did not mean "The absolute right to do whatever we please, regardless of our religion, our duties, or our neighbors."

The Founding Fathers of the United States looked at true freedom as obedience to moral laws. They did not seek to distance themselves from moral obligations, payments of debts, or the courts. Lawful freedom was "The right of decent people, governed by conscience, to make their own principal choices in life." This denotes a sensible, well-defined freedom anchored by government. The underlying theme is to establish a regulated, moderate, respectful freedom.

Freedom in America gives people clear political rights. Legal and political freedoms are the results of long struggles to gain rights in choosing one's way to live, work, and worship. In politics, freedom goes hand in hand with order and justice.

In private life, freedom gains stability through moderation, common sense, and respect for sound authority. Moral freedom connotes the ability to distinguish between right and wrong. This refers to "freedom of the will." Opposing this concept is the deterministic view that human beings act according to heredity, environment, and fate. Religious beliefs across many cultures and civilizations, however, foster the ideal that spontaneity comes from within, and people can make smart choices between differing plans of right and wrong. Samuel Johnson remarked in the 1700s, "All argument is against freedom of the will, all necessity is for it."

Democratic freedom is more than making choices for the individual or group; it also includes the freedom to share in setting up possible choices. This implies input from other sources, and a certain degree of restriction. Freedom gains temper with wise authority, and a justice system ruled by courts of law.

The balanced liberty of the United States that respects well-defined authority can be called "ordered liberty" or "ordered freedom." This means sustaining individual freedom by recognizing an orderly way of life. The Constitution is a document of ordered freedom. True political and ethical freedoms depend on justice, order, and the rules necessary to coexist peacefully with others.

Justice protects the life, property, rights, and dignity of the individual. Order makes justice possible by forming a moral law and upright authority. Order ensures that freedom for one is freedom for all. It is most interesting to note that freedom is not bestowed upon a people—it is created by individuals and communities.

The American Democracy
★★★

Democracy means rule by the people. It is a way of life. True democracy recognizes rights—that all people are equal before the law. American democracy first took shape in traditions carried to North America by the early English colonists. The Pilgrims, in 1620 Massachusetts, joined in the Mayflower Compact to "Enact, constitute, and frame such just and equal laws."

As the American Revolution spawned, the colonists were protesting the violations of taxation without representation, and the need for local government. The Declaration of Independence offered a new way of life in establishing an ideal maxim of human rights by which governments are to be guided. Life, liberty and the pursuit of happiness are unalienable rights.

At the time of its signing, The Declaration of Independence was seen as a daring experiment in government. In addition, The United States Constitution and Bill of Rights were hailed as inspired democratic documents of self-government and fundamental human freedoms. The theory of constitutional government involved the ideas of a limited government, with balanced executive, legislative, and judicial powers.

An open-door policy of equal opportunity brought people from all over the world to America. As the nation grew, a pioneer spirit of westward movement evolved with its spirit rooted in self-reliance, individual liberty, and the right to improve one's economic life. In this economic democracy, the guiding principle is that every person has a chance to improve their standing. This philosophy encourages private efforts to bolster equality and equal opportunity for all.

Of primary significance, is the point that drawing up democratic documents or laws does not guarantee a democracy's success. People must work continually for democratic freedom. Citizens need to be informed and able to act on their knowledge. Leaders in a democracy must gain the people's trust and act for their benefit. Education symbolizes the strength of a democracy by allowing an open forum of learning. Acknowledging the views of others is at the heart of a democracy, as are the concepts of respect, cooperation, and fair play.

Free Market Enterprise System
★★★

Freedom of enterprise is a major concept relevant to all other freedoms. A free enterprise system incorporates the following conditions: the means of production are privately owned and controlled; each person is free to make his or her own decisions in economic life; and each person's income is basically proportional to what one's labor and resources produce. In other words, what we call capitalism is simply a right to develop, own, and control one's destiny.

The free enterprise system in America did not develop from a deliberate plan. In the early American colonies, Great Britain had placed considerable control over the economic life of the people, with policies grounded in European Mercantilism. This government decided what its citizens should consume, produce and earn. Additionally, it specified where they should work and invest their money. These restrictions and the discontent they produced, led to the Revolutionary War in America.

Free enterprise arose as a reaction against government's control of economic life. The central ideas as stated in the 1776 book, *The Wealth of Nations*, by Adam Smith, support the belief that "The interests of the Nation are best served by permitting each person to make their own decisions and follow their own self-interest in economic life."

In a free enterprise system, the consumer is the chief object of attention. Profits and losses are statements reflecting what consumers want and consider useful. Efficient production by a skilled workforce is the goal.

Central freedoms in this system include, the freedom of job choice; private ownership of the means of production; unencumbered distribution of income; and open competition. All these facets point to one result, and the objective of business organizations—offering more for less. When a system of free people making free decisions in economic life, using some of the world's richest natural resources come together, economic progress and growth flourish.

Chapter Two

INDIVIDUALISM and PROGRESS
★★★
Theories of Business Organizations

Examining the cultural value systems inherent within American society and applying them to the workplace, are tasks requiring an expansive outlook on the composition and interaction of complex parts. Viewing the business entity as a small society, points to understanding the underlying value systems and operational requirements influencing productivity. Organizational behavior is the term used to describe the business relationship between people and progress.

The theories and research on how organizations function are the products of a system's perspective, where interdependent parts and outside forces regulate efficiency. Adopting a causal-correlation approach to analyzing organizations broadens the extent of objectivity and interpretation.

When practicing organizational diagnosis based on open systems theory, the premise is that organizations are microsystems with interrelated socio-technical functions, subjected to internal instability, and external environmental forces of customers, suppliers, competitors, and regulators. This socio-technical matrix is divided into managerial, psycho-social, technical, and structural subsystems. In further dissecting this model, the overall business climate constitutes a function of leadership behavior, role clarification, job characteristics, and organizational structure.

Initiating change in a subsystem can create a ripple effect across boundaries, affecting the organization as a whole. The sovereign criteria, or outputs, reflect the mission, goals, and values of the organization. Survival, productivity, effectiveness, and satisfaction are all outcomes influenced by the interaction of system inputs.

Given the changing nature of businesses (especially within their environment, task structure, and human resources), organization development practitioners constantly face reevaluation. Organizational theory has few axioms. Allowing constructive criticism in methodology and application opens the door to new patterns of management.

Theorists point to an existing "force field" between functions, and in relation to cultural, economic, and political demands. The organization achieves stability by adapting to these forces. In addition, integrating the needs of individuals with organizational and societal values, establishes a bond conducive to longevity and efficiency.

Loosely-coupled systems theory takes a slightly different posture on the structural and interpersonal dynamics of organizations. This hypothesis conveys separateness in functions, and desire for self-determination. For example, educational institutions operate in a semi-autonomous state, somewhat unresponsive to external policy and internal communication. In general, organizations are not the rational, tightly structured entities that researchers and theorists envision.

System interaction implies motivation. Viewing motivation as the impetus within organizations presents considerable opportunities and challenges. Focusing on the psycho-social system with the theory that attention to this subsystem will regulate performance, reflects a logical progression from past mechanical models of productivity to current value-related prototypes.

In a definitive study, *The Social Psychology of Organizations*, authors Katz and Kahn outline the bases of social systems as comprising "The role behaviors of members, the norms prescribing and sanctioning these behaviors and the values in which the norms are embedded...each behavioral element in the pattern is to a large extent caused and secured by the other."

Roles, norms and values vary in their degree of abstractness. Examining roles can provide a greater degree of interpretation and resolution. Gaining a clear perspective on clarifying individual roles has been problematic to social psychologists due to the complexity of this synthetic concept. The historical emphasis on the concept of role has centered on norm development, social interaction, participation, and innovative behavior.

Realizing the intricacy of decoding behavior and attitudes encourages organizational theorists to expand their vision, and search for more predictive variables. Handling individual differences and the unpredictable nature of human acts, requires a further dissection of motivational theory into operational components and contingencies.

Theories of Motivation
★★★

On a basic level, individuals are self-motivated to satisfy needs, wants, and aspirations. Maslow referred to these motivators as a "hierarchy of needs" encompassing physiological, safety, social, esteem, and self-actualization levels. Herzberg categorized human behavior from a perception of "hygienic" and "enrichment" factors.

Within an organizational context, individuals enter a company with different experiences, skills, and personal history. Being able to define the employee's role, while matching it to meaningful goals, depends on a plan both intuitive and structured.

Expectancy theory of motivation reinforces this viewpoint by providing a cause and effect methodology. A multivariate function emerges correlating effort, performance, and satisfaction. Individuals have expectations that effort will lead to performance; that performance will be instrumental for the attainment of some outcome; and that this outcome (reward) will be a positive match to the individual's needs, resulting in satisfaction.

In favoring this expectancy model, it is important for organizations to understand the goals of individuals, and facilitate the accomplishment of these goals. This model is an extension of path-goal leadership theory, supporting the premise that management behavior and organizational structure influence worker productivity.

In looking at the climate surrounding the work environment, arousal theory of motivation examines the relationship between stress and performance. Research suggests that at the optimum level of arousal, performance is at its highest level. Underutilization or overload induces increased stress (by increasing or decreasing exertion on the job), lowering levels of performance. The implications are that organizations need to alter job characteristics, and increase the individual's ability to perform the task. This can take place through effective leadership, and insightful training and development programs.

Accounting for individual differences accentuates the need to examine the person-environment fit. Studies indicate that individuals vary in their preference for stimulation. Hence, finding the right individual for the job may take preference over redesigning the job.

Equity theory of motivation complements the expectancy framework by examining the exchange relationship between employee and employer, where the worker's perceived contributions (inputs) match to the company's rewards (outcomes). Of principal significance, is the notion that individuals calculate their input/outcome ratio as it relates to other workers. This relationship is under constant evaluation for fairness, especially as it relates to other workers within and outside the organization.

In taking equity theory to a new level, there is also the position that establishing equity is a two-phase activity. Not only do individuals make comparisons with "referent others," but they keep a mental scorecard reflecting how they are treated on the job. Therefore, the first-order determinants of equity focus on the in-house exchange relationship between employer and employee. Second-level factors concentrate on a "comparative other" analysis.

From a broad vantage, sociologists assert that equity and reciprocity are universal norms. Psychologists like to explain these values in terms of personality balance and consistent behavior. In the text, *Social Behavior: Its Elementary Forms*, Homans puts forth the concept of distributive justice favoring the input/outcome comparison method. Adams (*Toward an Understanding of Inequity*) integrates these ideas, stating that individuals conceptually monitor and evaluate exchange relationships. This relationship may exist between individuals and organizations, as well as interpersonally. Equity or inequity, are processes that depend on inputs invested and outcomes (rewards) received.

Organizational theorists perceive the existence of a general force field (Lewin, *Field Theory in Social Science*) between individuals and organizations. Integrating the values and needs of each party establishes a bond contributing to efficiency and effectiveness. March and Simon use the terminology "inducements-contribution balance" in the book, *Organizations,* to express the psychological contract inherent within employer-employee relationships, in which individuals exchange behaviors for incentives.

These behaviors correspond to inputs. Incentives are a form of outcomes or rewards. In the text *Compensation Administration,* Belcher succinctly classifies inputs as job related contributions, performance related contributions, and personal ethics. Outcomes classify into extrinsic (pay/benefits) and intrinsic (recognition) rewards.

According to Adams (*Inequity in Social Exchange*), inputs and outcomes must satisfy two conditions to be evaluative within the exchange relationship—they must be recognized by one or both parties, and considered relevant. Furthermore, the research suggests that individuals weigh, sum, and evaluate their inputs/outputs in degrees of personal importance.

When this information is unclear, the individual chooses a comparison person as a point of reference. Hence, this external comparison standard serves as a corollary relationship when the individual's self-concept of job worth cannot be accurately evaluated.

In *Pay and Organizational Effectiveness,* Lawler uses these theories to explain pay satisfaction as a function of the congruence between what individuals perceive they are paid, and their perception of the amount they desire to be paid.

The amount of pay that should be received depends on perceived personal job inputs, job characteristics, and inputs/outcomes for a referent other.

Hamner and Harnett (*Goal-setting Performance, and Satisfaction in an Interdependent Task*), conclude that there is a marginally low level of difference in satisfaction between individuals who exceed either their personal goal, or the performance level of a referent other, or meet both conditions. The research predicts that individuals, who meet one or both of these situations, will experience high levels of performance and productivity.

These findings point toward creating a significant work experience. Workers who receive fair compensation, allowed self-determination on the job, and given an environment of support, are less likely to look outside the organization for information.

Clarifying the Role of the Individual
★★★

In bringing together the various theories and concepts relating to motivation, an aggregate model takes shape, helping define the role of the individual and the organization's ability to influence productivity.

<u>External Environment</u>
Customers, Suppliers, Competitors, Regulators

⇩

<u>Leadership Behavior</u>
Managerial Subsystem

⇕

<u>Role Clarification</u>
Psycho-Social Subsystem

⇕   <u>**Equity**</u>

⇩

Effort ------------------➤ *Performance*----➤ *Rewards*----➤ *Satisfaction*

⇕
<u>Job Characteristics</u>
Technical Subsystem

⇕
<u>Organizational Structure</u>
Structural Subsystem

Figure 1   A Conceptual Framework of Employee Motivation

Figure 1 outlines a general system's framework of motivation, with expectancy and equity theories serving as the foundation. By isolating the subsystem of role clarification, it is evident that this variable is an interrelated function of job characteristics, organizational structure and leadership behavior.

Regarding the key job characteristics for work design, Hackman and Oldham's *Motivation Through the Design of Work* identifies the following:

Skill Variety: Requiring a variety of different activities in carrying out the work; involving a number of an individual's skills and talents.

Task Identity: Requiring completion of a whole and identifiable piece of work; doing a job from beginning to end with a visible outcome.

Task Significance: The job has a substantial impact on the lives or work of other people—whether in the immediate organization or external environment.

Autonomy: Providing substantial independence, freedom, and discretion to the individual in scheduling work, and determining the procedures in carrying it out.

Feedback: Obtaining direct and clear information about the effectiveness of the individual's performance as it relates to job requirements.

In addition, major elements of an organization's structure have a distinct impact on motivating employees and constructing an efficient operation. Researchers Nadler, Hackman, and Lawler outline the primary structural components in the text, *Managing Organizational Behavior.* These include:

Composition of units: Defining what roles or positions are grouped together into work and larger units.

Reporting relationships: Specifying which individuals or groups are accountable and report to others.

Design of tasks and roles: Relating to how different positions are designated—including job content, position demands, and decision-making authority.

Communication patterns: Reflecting the movement of information between and within different units.

Measurement and information systems: Representing formal systems to collect and distribute information about organizational functioning.

Reward systems: Set up as formal mechanisms to provide incentives.

Selection, placement, and development systems: Instituted as procedures for attracting, hiring, and promoting members.

Putting it All Together
★★★

It will be important for leaders of organizations to provide a work environment incorporating meaningful job characteristics, and a structure benefiting the mission of worker satisfaction. Leadership behavior is the glue holding together the business entity. The ability to positively guide and influence the work of employees is the key to forging a successful workplace.

When managers design jobs that offer challenge, significance, and independent decision making; workers become self-motivated, leading to enhanced levels of performance. Improving task skills through insightful training and development programs serves as a catalyst in aiding the individual's career path. Providing for an open forum of discussion about performance standards, helps solve problems and achieve higher levels of productivity.

Gearing structural design toward maximizing organizational efficiency requires a clear mission statement, well-defined reporting relationships, creative group processes, and means to implement a plan of action. In addition, favoring open patterns of communication between units and departments brings about innovative ideas and solutions. Being able to monitor and measure company accomplishments aids in developing equitable reward systems, and designing practical jobs. Setting up diverse channels for the recruiting, selection, and retention of employees, champions a system ingrained with equality, equity, and ethical behavior.

In summary, individualism is an intricate concept, far more involved than giving independence to the worker. Because organizations comprise many parts, giving self-determination to employees relies on the careful analysis and implementation of social and technical systems. Clarifying the role of the individual is the primary spotlight of organizations, as it is the defining aspect in determining success or failure.

Chapter Three

EQUALITY and EQUITY
★★★

Overview

The norms of equality and egalitarianism are deeply implanted statutes in American life. Civil Rights, Equal Opportunity, and Affirmative Action are covenants with a long history of struggle and acceptance. Discrimination and prejudice are behaviors and attitudes still under remediation. There is a constant need to address issues surrounding inequality, and strive for uniform standards of social justice.

Without delving into the chronology of equal rights in America, it is simple to state that these universal values are critical to the advancement of American business in the twenty-first century. Employment discrimination has gained considerable attention over the years, as it relates to race, gender, religion, national origin, handicap, age, and military service. Labor law has rendered decisions addressing employment practices in the areas of recruiting, selection, promotion, wages, union relations, safety/health, and benefits.

Of all the issues surrounding the equality question, the most significant topic facing corporate America today is the condition of pay equity. This norm supersedes all other economic concerns, in that it lies at the heart of worker motivation and satisfaction. The right to secure an honest wage has repercussions extending from the realms of relieving poverty, to advancing productivity. The importance of not only satisfying basic human needs, but furnishing a high quality of life, are primary objectives of a fully functioning society.

In an era where the minimum wage has been stagnant for over a decade, and the right to a "living wage" is more fiction than fact, the time has come for new dimensions in defining the concept of job worth. Franklin Delano Roosevelt concisely stated:

> No business which depends for existence on paying less than living wages to its workers, has any right to continue in this country.

Thanks to initiatives by the American Friends Service Committee, National Council of Churches USA, and Association of Community Organizations for Reform Now, strides are being made to upgrade the minimum wage on a state-by-state basis. The "Let Justice Roll" campaign, in issuing a report entitled, *A Just Minimum Wage: Good for Workers, Business, and Our Future*, dictates that raising the minimum wage is:

> An economic imperative for the enduring strength of our workforce, businesses, communities, and the economy, as well as a moral imperative for the very soul of our nation.

In going beyond the basic entitlement of a living wage, the chief contention facing organizations is the issue of pay equity. This matter addresses the need to fully examine job worth, and provide for an objective, unbiased valuation. According to United States Department of Labor data, the average worker has not seen a decent pay increase despite a strong economy and significant productivity gains.

In a 2006 workplace attitude survey by staffing agency Randstad USA, with Harris Interactive Inc., 39 percent of employees think their companies pay less-than-market-rate salaries. This figure compares with 28 percent for the previous year. The survey notes:

> While an increased number of employers think their compensation practices are on par, more employees believe they are underpaid, signaling a widening split between employers and employees about what constitutes competitive pay. Far and away, employees say the top benefit related to happiness is competitive pay. Companies continue to fall short on delivering on these most-valued benefits. Surprisingly, only 49 percent of employers say they offer competitive pay. The discrepancy between the need for competitive pay and its existence makes it clear employers must do a better job at managing compensation to keep employees motivated and happy.

The National Committee on Pay Equity is a coalition of women's and civil rights organizations working to eliminate gender-and race-based wage discrimination. Its purpose is to close the wage gap, especially as it affects women and minorities. The Bureau of Labor Statistics 2004 research findings (collected by the Institute for Women's Policy), and the General Accounting Office's 2003 report, *Women's Earnings*, found that the wage gap still exceeds 20 percent, even when considering demographic and work-related factors such as occupation, industry, race, marital status, and job tenure.

The National Committee on Pay Equity is deeply involved in creating awareness and gaining enforcement of pay equity legislation. The Committee points to Ontario, Canada, and their 1988 Pay Equity Act—the first law requiring public and private sector employers to implement pay equity. Within the United States, on the federal level, the Fair Pay Act of 2005 has been introduced in the U.S. House of Representatives, and U.S. Senate. According to the Committee:

> Fair pay for employees can lead to greater productivity by raising morale among workers who expect to receive fair pay for their work. By compensating workers for the fair value of their work, the Fair Pay Act can help businesses recruit and retain the best-qualified workers. There has been no evidence of job loss associated with any pay equity plans. Pay equity can bring great savings to taxpayers at a minimal cost to business. Pay equity helps workers become self-sufficient and reduces their reliance on government assistance programs. The Act will provide businesses with an incentive to examine their wage-setting policies in order to eliminate any bias.

Introduction to Pay Equity
★★★

The issue of pay equity concerns the concept of equal pay for work of equal value. This orientation is an extension of the Fair Labor Standards Act of 1938, and the Equal Pay Act of 1963, calling for equal pay for equal work. Pay equity principles also further the Civil Rights Act of 1964 (Title VII), prohibiting wage discrimination based on sex, race, or national origin, especially involving jobs predominately held by women and minorities. Simply stated, pay equity is a system comparing equivalent, not identical jobs.

When looking closely at the fundamentals of pay equity, specific considerations arise such as individual motivation, organizational commitment, and increased productivity. Equity theory of motivation states that individuals compare their ratio of inputs and outcomes (rewards) to others within and outside their organization. When these comparisons are equal, the individual experiences satisfaction, leading to higher levels of effort and performance. There is also evidence that individuals evaluate their own contributions and rewards, apart from others. The significance of these considerations to employers and employees encourages a deeper analysis of the concept of pay equity.

Achieving pay equity is a complex procedure that depends on proper design and implementation functions. For organizations to establish pay equity practices, the key is vigilance to design instruments, such as job evaluation and market survey data; as well as the capable implementation and administration of these elements.

Most studies of pay equity have paid close attention to job evaluation techniques, specifically the determination of compensable job factors and their potential for bias. The utilization of market survey data, and concern toward the administration of "comparable worth" plans, however, have received less emphasis.

Viewing pay equity as a two-phase process points to understanding the interrelationship between design and implementation activities. If pay equity is to become a viable issue, control mechanisms must develop alongside technical solutions. Joint-cooperation between employers, employees, and regulating agencies serves as a complementary function to research and design practices.

The Design of Pay Equity
★★★

In a *Labor Law Journal* article, entitled "Comparable Worth: Recent Developments in Selected States," pay equity is defined as:

> A concept calling for measuring the relative values to the employer of disparate jobs, specifically those done by men and those done by women, through the application of job evaluation, and other systems that so far as possible eliminate sex bias by attaching objective weights consistently across job families to factors inherent in the determination of gradations of skill, effort, responsibility and working conditions.

The main problems in operationalizing this definition, as determined by the National Academy of Sciences (in an interim report to the Equal Employment Opportunity Commission), concern the subjective judgments about job content; the choosing and weighting of compensable factors; and the use of multiple job evaluation plans within a single firm. Despite these limitations, the Committee on Occupational Classification and Analysis of the National Research Council, found job evaluation to be potentially useful as employers and employees mutually decide on evaluation criteria.

The Committee reported that no strictly scientific basis for determining job worth exists. Although the idea of establishing "bona fide compensable factors" may be problematic; relating skill, effort, responsibilty, and working conditions as outlined under The Equal Pay Act is the preferred method.

The courts have held that job evaluation procedures must accurately reflect job content and be detail oriented.

Employers can follow the guidelines for job analysis and employee selection, taking a similar role in the development and utilization of equitable job evaluation plans.

Data collection should include interviews with incumbents, supervisors, and administrators; information from training manuals; observed on-the-job performance; and the use of questionnaires and checklists. Data collection is to be performed by an expert job analyst, and from a large sample. Information identified through job analysis should focus on elements, aspects, characteristics, aptitudes, knowledge, skills, ability, and critical incidents.

A concern toward establishing accurate job evaluation plans stems from court rulings that infer the absence of a job evaluation plan is a sign of employment discrimination. In a landmark 1981 case (County of Washington [Oregon] v. Gunther), the Supreme Court ruled that Title VII of the Civil Rights Act covers wage discrimination even if jobs are different. Additionally, The Court ruled that conducting a job evaluation survey, but failing to follow it in setting wage rates may constitute evidence of intent to discriminate.

Because of these discrimination cases, the use of advanced statistical programs such as multiple regression analysis are gaining greater acceptance by organizations. There has been a recent shift away from non-quantitative, narrative, job description methods toward quantitative point-factor and factor analysis systems of job evaluation. This change has emerged due to the system's ease of use, technical adequacy, and acceptance by affected personnel.

A quantitative approach to job evaluation helps measure the inputs of employees and determine the corresponding pay level. The concept of internal equity states that individuals are equitably paid if the ratio of their inputs and pay are basically equal to a comparative other's ratio (within the same organization). Therefore, accurately measuring the relative value of jobs within an organization is the primary task of job evaluation.

The design of pay equity plans also examines the notion of external equity. This concept states that individuals make input/pay comparisons across different organizations. The individual's perception of equity is a complicated issue, and one that employers are giving greater attention. Factors such as company policy, internal labor dynamics, job classification, job level, and union membership all influence an individual's perception of equity. For example, workers in relatively open internal labor markets, as well as professionals, mobile middle managers, crafts workers, and union members, tend to make external wage comparisons.

This orientation indicates that a system of evaluating jobs accounts for both internal and external measures of equity. Utilizing market survey data is a good means of establishing external equity, while also serving as a logical complement to job evaluation techniques and the preservation of internal equity.

Regarding market survey data, the consensus is that these surveys perpetuate wage discrimination against women and minorities, and are difficult to correct. Long-term employment discrimination in hiring, training, and promotion has created segmented labor markets and suppressed wages. It is for these reasons that a renewed interest in job evaluation is surfacing, with the realization that pay equity is an issue confronting both wage and employment discrimination.

Despite these built-in inequities, the courts have ruled in cases of pay equity that market rates *do* provide a legitimate explanation for differences in wages. The employer is not liable for marketplace conditions it did not create. Given this status, pay equity advocates will have to acknowledge market survey data; while at the same time reinforce their position on employment discrimination relating to recruiting, selection, training, and promotion.

From a functional viewpoint, market survey data works conjunctively with job evaluation methods. Even if a thorough job evaluation program is undertaken, the results need to anchor with the external labor market, establishing dollar values. Concentrating on key or benchmark jobs across job families helps create wage rates for non-benchmark positions.

In the Minority Report of the Committee on Occupational Classification and Analysis, member Ernest J. McCormick stated:

> To develop a job evaluation system that did not first examine (and compare) the content of jobs, and second, relate the job content to a value system that underlies our entire economy is not realistic, practical, or economically or socially feasible.

From a broad perspective, the true purpose of a job evaluation program is to create a system in accord with the external labor market, avoiding inflated internal labor market costs. In addition, the system aids in the attraction, retention, and motivation of employees. Using both job evaluation techniques and market survey data are steps toward achieving cost effectiveness for the organization, and pay equity for its individual members.

The Implementation of Pay Equity
★★★

In turning pay equity design considerations into practice, complementary administrative functions are necessary to ensure the system's efficiency and survival. Proponents of pay equity argue that current job evaluation systems are outdated, subject to bias, and in need of upgrading. This concern points to providing an open forum for the review and development of job evaluation plans.

The Committee on Occupational Classification and Analysis supports these claims in concluding that wage discrimination is widespread; existing wage rates need to be revalued (although no universal standard of job worth exists); and employers and employees should agree on measures of job value determination. The Committee recommends utilizing job evaluation techniques, as this practice is prevalent throughout American business and the advanced industrialized world.

As a first step, organizations should enforce The Equal Pay Act, Title VII of the Civil Rights Act, and Executive Order 11246 (relating to contractors), the federal statutes prohibiting wage discrimination. Staff and officials committed to enforcing these statutes are to be appointed at the local, state, and federal levels. This includes positions in the U.S. Department of Justice, Office of Federal Contract Compliance Program, Equal Employment Opportunity Commission (EEOC), and the Office of Personnel Management.

Pay equity programs can be implemented either by the federal government, local governments working with business and labor unions, or voluntary compliance by private employers.

Some consider the federal government through guidelines of the Equal Employment Opportunity

Commission to be the preferable solution, while others note past problems with enforcement and administration of wage discrimination issues. Recent proposals to secure pay equity legislation recognize these past weaknesses, and stress a strong national commitment to the practice of pay equity. For example, the proposed 2005 Fair Pay Act directs the Equal Employment Opportunity Commission to:

> Undertake studies and provide information and technical assistance to employers, labor organizations, and the general public concerning effective means available to implement the Act; and carry on a continuing program of research, education, and technical assistance with specified components related to the purposes of this Act.

Over the years, job evaluation practices applicable to federal workers have been examined by two Executive Branch agencies at the request of Congress. The General Accounting Office has looked at the overall federal compensation system, while the Office of Personnel Management has studied the point factor/factor analysis system. This Factor Evaluation System has been developed in conjunction with managers, employees, and other participating groups who sat in with the classification authority as evaluation and qualification standards were set. This system has produced positive responses from employers and employees.

State and local governments have addressed the pay equity issue by sponsoring hearings or research projects, to collect information on other governments' comparable worth activities. Involving interested constituencies, and providing information on the degree of wage discrimination are important components of this approach.

In regard to state and local government initiatives, most states currently have statutes on equal pay similar to the

Equal Pay Act. Twenty-one states passed equal pay laws before the federal law. This situation of whether some states are moving ahead of federal law, also applies to the pay equity matter. State departments of personnel management are being directed through bills to examine the equal pay for work of equal value issue. Twenty states have made some adjustments of wages, correcting for gender and racial bias. Seven of these states fully implemented pay equity programs.

Job evaluation studies have been completed in several states ranging from small projects to large studies. Joint committees consisting of workers' representatives, advocacy groups, unions, and management, directed these studies. They have been initiated by means of collective bargaining, legislation, executive order budget appropriation, and civil service department activities.

Unions have become actively involved in the pay equity issue. In many cases, collective bargaining has produced positive results. Unions have hired expert job evaluators, and through arbitration upgraded salaries. There has been an attempt to negotiate across-the-board dollar increases, rather than on a percentage basis, to close the wage gap.

Unions have also conducted their own wage and job studies. Depending on findings of the study and union strength, lobbying or bargaining for a joint labor-management job evaluation review usually follows. For example, the job evaluation plan of the State of Washington was upgraded due to intensive lobbying by state employees (American Federation of State, County, and Municipal Employees) and their union. Pay equity was implemented over an eight-year period, at a modest cost of 2.6 percent of the state's personnel budget. In the State of Minnesota, progressive pay equity legislation gave raises to thirty-thousand employees, at a cost of only 3.7 percent of the state's payroll budget, over a four-year span.

A prime case study of pay equity occurred in the State of Oregon during the 1980s, where a complete restructuring of the State's classification and compensation system was carried out over a seven-year period, involving more than thirty-four thousand workers. Utilizing point-factor job evaluation methods (developed by an outside consulting agency, and agreed upon by union members and management), pay equity upgrades totaled more than 52 million dollars. This massive undertaking was not without its limitations, as participants found it necessary to move from a phase of "expert" analysis to one of "mobilizing" strategies.

Margaret Hallock, Chair of the Oregon Task Force on State Compensation and Classification Equity, voiced concern over the research methods:

> Job evaluation is a double-edged sword in while it can yield concrete evidence of a pay gap and raise consciousness about discrimination, it is a cumbersome and expensive management tool that is often biased against women and can inhibit collective bargaining. . . . Job evaluation turns key political decisions and issues of value into a technical discussion. Questions of rights and values are sidetracked into issues of appropriate techniques.

This apparent disconnect in the motives of labor and management pertaining to job evaluation policies, highlights the need for objective and acceptable measurement standards. Various job evaluation programs are products of external management consulting firms' research, and inconsistent with the inner workings of specific job sectors.

An example of gaining parity in pay equity is the private sector agreement between AT&T and the Communications Workers of America that established an Occupational Job Evaluation Committee. This Committee is comprised equally of union and management members. It is assembled to research, develop, and make recommendations relating to the design and implementation of a job evaluation plan that provides an equitable wage structure for all non-management workers.

In taking a proactive stance, unions can initiate pay equity standards through official union policy. The AFL-CIO has called upon its affiliated unions to work through contract negotiations in upgrading undervalued job classifications, and bring into practice joint union-employer pay equity studies to identify and correct inequities.

If collective bargaining and setting up joint committee structures fail, legal action is a recourse. The International Union of Electrical, Radio, and Machine Workers initiated a Title VII Compliance Program that educated union members and conducted research on job/wage comparisons by sex and race. If the employer refuses to bargain under this program, charges can be filed with the National Labor Relations Board, and complaints filed under Title VII.

Because unions have limited abilities to bargain for wages in the federal government, and some state or local governments, lobbying for legislation and guaranteed participation in the design and implementation of pay equity plans are aims of the National Committee on Pay Equity. Many unions are members of this Committee, whose primary purpose is to provide information, coordination, and strategy direction to organizations and individuals pursuing pay equity. Encouraging voluntary compliance by private employers, stimulating new pay equity activities, and providing an overall educational policy, are major goals of the organization.

The Committee has issued a pay equity self-audit for employers, derived from a document created by the U.S. Department of Labor Women's Bureau. A ten-step guide is available "To assist employers in analyzing their own wage-setting policies and establishing consistent and fair pay practices for all." The guide contains the following provisions:

1. Conduct a recruitment self-audit;
2. Evaluate your compensation system for internal equity;
3. Evaluate your compensation system for industry competitiveness;
4. Conduct a new job evaluation system if needed;
5. Examine your compensation system and compare job grades or scores;
6. Review data for personnel entering your company;
7. Assess opportunities for employees to win commissions and bonuses;
8. Assess how raises are awarded;
9. Evaluate employee training, development and promotion opportunities;
10. Implement changes where needed, maintain equity and share your success.

Conclusions
★★★

The attainment of pay equity is a complex issue requiring varied design and implementation approaches. Because organizations have firm-specific qualities, no universal standards of achieving pay equity are evident. Organizations examining their internal workings and external environment can create a pay equity plan ensuring equal pay for work of equal value.

For employees to understand the pay equity system and perceive it to be fair, coordination in designing job evaluation instruments and their adequate administration is necessary. Without enhanced levels of communication, trust remains low, resulting in poor acceptance of the pay equity plan.

As a first measure, the organization's adherence to Title VII of the Civil Rights Act of 1964, prohibits wage discrimination on the basis of sex, race, and national origin. Adopting pay equity principles also assumes familiarity with the Equal Pay Act of 1963, requiring equal pay for equal work, based on the criteria of effort, skill, responsibility, and working conditions. Abiding by these laws puts the organization in a position to understand the premise of comparable worth.

The concept of pay equity is an intriguing one, and still not completely understood. Equity theory of motivation notes that individuals measure their ratio of inputs and outcomes to others. Being able to quantify inputs of the individual, and assign reward levels, are major problems confronting pay equity practitioners. In addition, it is unclear whether individuals make comparisons strictly within their organization (internal) or outside of it (external). The choice of a reference person depends on several personal, job-related, and internal labor market factors.

In that pay equity concerns individual motivation and increased productivity for the organization, accounting for both internal and external measures of equity are the logical choices. Taking this stance necessitates using both job evaluation techniques to measure internal equity, as well as market survey data to evaluate external equity. When employers account for individual differences among employees' perceptions of pay equity, a comprehensive compensation system is in place.

Job evaluation plans that are detail-oriented, and reflect job worth, ensure objectivity in design. Favoring a quantitative approach and expertly analyzing evaluation criteria support a commitment to accuracy. After the careful choosing, weighting, and accumulating of point factors, it becomes necessary to relate these results to the external labor market. Identifying key jobs common to the organization and its competitive environment, preserves external equity, avoiding inflated internal labor costs.

When a pay equity system encompasses internal and external measures of equity, the employer takes a stand against discrimination; adheres to standards favored by the courts; and produces a wage policy increasing morale and productivity.

In attacking the proper design of pay equity, the strategies of gaining plan acceptance and considering implementation measures early in the process, are of primary importance. From the onset, pay equity activities strive to involve parties and constituents represented by the plan. This exercise depends on the organization's environment, and whether any policy-setting issues involve collective bargaining contracts. Employers, employees, union representatives, and other regulating agencies form a consensual base in developing pay equity practices. Mutually agreed standards of evaluation, as well as periodic review of these measures help eliminate bias and increase trust toward the system.

Because of the difficulty in monitoring pay equity on a national level, local initiatives and voluntary action by concerned parties take preference. Pay equity advocates realize that the Equal Pay Act of 1963 took years to become actively enforced, and still is not faithfully practiced by many employers.

Given this position, pay equity legislation concentrates on effective administration and advanced educational programs. Appointment of legislative and administrative staff members committed to pay equity is of primary importance. Emphasizing state and local government initiatives, through collective bargaining and joint labor-management job evaluation committees, aids in the implementation of comparable worth platforms.

Voluntary compliance by private employers also furthers pay equity by setting up experimental programs. Refusal by employers to become involved in such a system necessitates appropriate action, and potential lawsuits.

The proposed Fair Pay Act of 2005 is a prime example of reaching accountability in pay equity. The Act allows each employer to decide how its employees are paid, requiring a non-discriminatory system for setting wages. The Act does make exceptions for different wage rates based on seniority, merit, and quality or quantity of work. Concerning enforcement, the Act allows class action lawsuits, as well as compensatory and punitive damages. It also requires some employers to disclose to the EEOC general job classifications and pay statistics, while retaining individual confidentiality. The Act prohibits lowering any employee's wage rate in order to achieve fair pay.

Regarding the issues of disclosure and reporting, the National Committee on Pay Equity reasons:

For a free enterprise system to work effectively, all economic decision-makers require information for fully informed choices. This includes employees. Currently, employers are entitled to know a great deal about employees, but employees often lack even the most basic information about overall compensation practices. Without this information, workers cannot fairly compare and evaluate present and prospective employers, thus artificially constraining their employment choices. Disclosure will aid employers as well. Analyzing compensation statistics by job type, gender, race, and national origin will enable employers to identify and remedy inequities that might not otherwise come to their attention. Fair employers have nothing to hide.

Explaining policies on pay equity contributes to employee motivation and satisfaction, by helping workers evaluate their job inputs and rewards, as posited by equity theory. In looking at a broad framework, pay equity starts from an educational perspective. Establishing policies on pay equity within company training and development programs, as well as educating the public through publications and conferences, give greater attention to the issue of fair pay, and help eliminate wage discrimination. Specifying aims of the program, with an emphasis on justice, elimination of poverty, and improved productivity, are goals common to all individuals.

Opponents of pay equity cite increased costs in developing design and implementation functions, in addition to inflated labor costs. If pay equity does indeed reflect human motivation, these costs will be more than offset by increased morale, performance, and worker satisfaction. Pay equity is therefore, ultimately an issue of national productivity, increased standards of living, and the right for all individuals to a just society.

If we are to go forward, we must go back and rediscover those precious values—that all reality hinges on moral foundations and that all reality has spiritual control.

Dr. Martin Luther King, Jr.

Chapter Four

ETHICS and MORALITY
★★★

Introduction to Ethics

Ethics is a moral philosophy studying human behavior as it relates to voluntary actions bearing upon right and wrong. Ethics is a systematic science of conduct, whereas morality refers to the patterns and rules of acting in a proper way. The merging of private and public ethical issues is central to the American democracy, especially as it influences community welfare.

When talking about ethics and morality, the principles surrounding the Golden Rule set a good example of treating people fairly, and showing concern for others in need. Within a business context, the helping relationship increases profitability and aids in the growth of employees. Extending this view into the community in a humanitarian way, brings triumph to the underprivileged, and administers sympathy to those in distress. Business ethicists like to use the term "balanced scorecard" to describe the link between financial performance and corporate social responsibility.

In formulating an ethics plan affecting the inner organizational workings and outside community, a careful, slow approach sets the tone. Walking a fine line in bringing people and culture together harmoniously is the wise course of action. Whether implementing a code of ethics, or humanitarian outreach program, a peaceful mission of friendship and hospitality is the aim. In garnering a "halo effect," the organization adopts a position favoring equality, respect, and social responsibility.

Business morality in America grew out of early religious ethics highlighting order, integrity, fair dealing, and the individual's place in society. The notion of truth, justice and the American way, points to honesty in people, products, and image. The charismatic organization captures and entertains a society of individuals through powerful communications, echoing a message of norms, values, and ecological issues. The idea of working communities is a good model to describe the modern idea of "living at work." In today's business world, it is imperative to break down barriers of traditional operational modes, and establish a free atmosphere of exchanging information.

What is Corporate Social Responsibility?
★★★

The World Business Council for Sustainable Development defines Corporate Social Responsibility (CSR) as "The commitment of business to contribute to sustainable economic development, working with employees, their families, the local community, and society-at-large to improve their quality of life." Furthermore, the Council notes that a clear strategy based on integrity, social values, and long-term commitment contributes to the well-being of society.

According to Social Venture Network, a community of business owners, investors, and nonprofit leaders; corporate social responsibility standards exemplify:

> A system of values based on our understanding of the points of contact between business and society. The values cover a wide range of contemporary social issues. What turns them into a system is the belief that business is an integral part of something greater than itself, an institution of society that performs an increasingly vital role in assuring the well-being of society's members.

Corporate social responsibility integrates social, economic, and environmental purposes in what devotees refer to as the "triple bottom line" of people, profits, and planet. It joins the concept of sustainable development. CSR is a crucial element in the corporate structure and way of doing business. It is a determining agent in leading the innovative organization. CSR is applicable to businesses of any size.

The words "transparency" and "accountability" often define the mood of a company, in relation to decision making, strategy, operations management, and cultural diversity. A comprehensive corporate social responsibility program helps organizations enhance growth, adapt to change, manage risk, improve performance, and stabilize the company's reputation. These favorable outcomes are goals beneficial to all the company's stakeholders—employees, unions, suppliers, customers, shareholders, regulators, and community.

Consumers and investors in today's world favor companies with a social conscience. In addition, the world community has put forth its guidelines and ideologies in the form of compacts by the United Nations, and Organization for Economic Cooperation and Development.

From a systems point of view, CSR helps smooth internal organizational workings, and satisfies requirements of external regulatory agencies. Beyond improving one's image, the CSR-involved company gains a competitive advantage in many areas—including opening up new markets; increasing operational efficiency through clear management policies; securing access to capital; strengthening supply chain relationships; and meeting legal regulations.

Outpacing the economic benefits, true corporate social responsibility practices are moral principles—closely aligned with the company's mission, value structure, and culture. Designing useful codes of conduct is an endeavor subject to constant assessment and valuation. Developing a cogent CSR program follows a path of defining the organization's goals, and gaining commitment from all interested parties toward implementing a sustainable plan.

Although seen as a voluntary practice, CSR is in reality an extension of the American democratic experience. It is fuel for entrepreneurship, economic expansion, equal opportunity, quality of life, and a healthy society.

By emphasizing a respect for human rights; concern for natural resource utilization; and encouragement of innovative solutions to improve performance; CSR has the potential to influence global patterns of productivity. The European Union looks at CSR as a focal point toward achieving long-term prosperity, solidarity, and security. Expressing a partnership of ideas within the organization, and extending this message to the community-at-large, portrays a society of like-minded individuals bound together by a sense of purpose.

On a worldly level, the United Nations *Global Compact* signifies a voluntary contract, addressing the issues of human rights, labor, and the environment. It is a "network" of ideas, actors, and facilitators engaging in bettering society. CSR supports the *International Bill of Human Rights,* which includes a set of inalienable rights protecting the dignity of every human being. These are rights of respect given to all, regardless of political or cultural orientation. The business entity acts as a mini-society, and in ideal terms, adheres to these universal norms when dealing with employees and the community.

The Caux Round Table, an organization comprising senior business leaders from Europe, Japan, and North America expresses a world standard of shared values and acceptable business behaviors:

> These principles are rooted in two basic ethical ideals: kyosei and human dignity. The Japanese concept of 'kyosei' means living and working together for the common good, enabling cooperation and mutual prosperity to coexist with healthy and fair competition. 'Human dignity' refers to the sacredness or value of each person as an end, not simply as a mean to the fulfillment of others' purposes or even majority prescription.

Regarding the practical applications of these principles, the Caux Round Table puts forth the following recommendations:

We believe in the dignity of every employee and in taking employee interests seriously. We therefore have a responsibility to:

- Provide jobs and compensation that improve workers' living conditions;

- Provide working conditions that respect each employee's health and dignity;

- Be honest in communications with employees and open in sharing information, limited only by legal and competitive constraints;

- Listen to and, where possible, act on employee suggestions, ideas, requests, and complaints;

- Engage in good faith negotiations when conflict arises;

- Avoid discriminatory practices and guarantee equal treatment and opportunity in areas such as gender, age, race, religion, and disability; and

- Encourage and assist employees in developing relevant and transferable skills and knowledge.

Corporate social responsibility reflects the dominant qualities of American democracy, serving as a self-governing mechanism promoting individual responsibility and civil rights. Although this definition connotes a blanket description of values, ethics, equality, and efficiency—CSR is really a formal declaration of intent and action. It is a wide-ranging statement, encapsulating divergent tenets of doing business. Vision and responsibility are imprints of an organization's philosophy, defining its personality and impact on others.

Matching values and behavior is often a difficult task for the young organization, or company implementing change. Projecting an image of social responsibility is one matter; while implementing and ingraining these ideals are very different endeavors. A commitment to CSR principles by all employees and company decision makers is the attitude requisite to achieving compliance. CSR is a united force, characterizing the ideology and actions of many individuals. Although a company's image and "responsibility quotient" personify the organization's disposition, this outlook is really a summation of individual ethical behaviors.

Allowing the free exchange of information throughout all departments of the firm, and making this information available to stakeholders, heightens the company's resolve toward ethical behavior. Education is the principal influence on organizational efficiency and effectiveness. Corporate social responsibility encourages an open forum of discussion and forthright disclosure—all with one intention—to improve the economic, social, and environmental lives of all concerned parties. CSR is the imprint of a company's core values.

Accordant with channels of communication are the platforms of continuing education and training. Providing employees with the necessary information to maximize their job performance within a socially responsible work environment can lead to "perspective transformation." Mezirow coined this term in explaining a theory of adult learning that permits, "a more inclusive and discriminating integration of experience," helping the individual, "research problems, build confidence, examine action alternatives, identify resources, anticipate consequences, and foster participation and leadership."

Integrating Corporate Social Responsibility
★★★

From a sociological viewpoint, making CSR part of a company's fabric follows the cumulative processes of integration—these are contact, cooperation, assimilation, and amalgamation. After introducing and "selling" the idea to managers, the program diffuses across all operational levels of the organization, and finally marries to the outside community. This continuing, experimental process strives toward perfection through constant practice and revaluation. Executive and employee education programs relating to CSR are requirements of the value-driven organization.

Establishing a formal committee of executives, employees, managers, and board members; acts in gathering accurate information, spreading policy, and advancing a strong corporate citizenship plan. Once a framework is in place, a functional unit takes charge of duties within the human resources department, reporting to the Chief Executive Officer, or Board.

Enacting a code of ethics is a logical step toward supporting full disclosure, fair dealing, compliance with laws, and protection of company assets. The actions necessary to fulfill this ethical statement include; honesty and forthrightness in communications, management leading by example, and teamwork. A code of ethics is understandable and applicable when results reflect behaviors and actions. Additionally, rules and regulations are relevant to the organization's products, size, and scope of operations.

In terms of public relations, good corporate citizenship helps minimize risk, and attract the best job candidates. CSR is an integral part of recruitment, selection, orientation, and retention practices, in substantiating a baseline of commitment to human welfare.

In relation to the marketplace, socially responsible companies target sales and advertising strategies with an honest, up-front style. Conveying the message of value in one's product or service not only implies dollars, but sense. Although price, quality, and service still motivate consumer-buying habits, the emotional or genuine message has major impact. The bottom line in understanding consumer behavior and achieving profitability is fusing societal values with the organization's mission and product line.

Increasing the intangible aspect of products or services represents improvements in quality. By optimizing working conditions through fair labor practices, productivity advances include reduced error rates and greater quality control. In retaining a more mature workforce, the company ensures consistency in output of goods and services. Total quality management programs include objective standards of measurement, reliability, performance, and feedback.

Organizations take a big step toward forming a positive impression with the public by embracing community outreach programs—centered in sustainable partnerships favoring volunteerism, education, charity, and enhancement. On a tangential level, environmental concerns for preserving the eco-system, and conserving natural resources, are essential platforms of socially responsible conduct.

Practice What You Preach
★★★

Corporate social responsibility is the face of any organization, company, or institution. It defines the reason for existence, in merging innovative products and services with societal concerns. Beyond providing a rewarding and inspiring work environment, CSR forms a bond with the community of suppliers, customers, neighbors, regulators, and investors. It stands for a global commitment to doing the right thing, and advancing civilization by supporting the universal values of helping others in need.

The research firm KPMG, identifies in a 2005 study, *International Survey of Corporate Responsibility Reporting*, the key reasons firms favor CSR programs. They are:

1. Economic considerations
2. Ethical considerations
3. Innovation and learning
4. Employee motivation
5. Risk management/Risk reduction
6. Access to capital/Increased shareholder value
7. Reputation/Brand
8. Market position/Share
9. Strengthened Supplier Relationships
10. Cost Savings

The fact that cost savings is a secondary consideration points to taking a long-term perspective on establishing a flexible plan. When ethics, innovation, learning, and motivation are dominant goals of organizations, economic prosperity rises to the top. Intermediary factors such as risk management, capital expenditure, and marketing strategies also gain strength, representing the backbone of the company.

CSR is a modern definition of democracy. Through a program favoring freedom of information and moral authority, American business can be the touchstone for ethical behavior and worldly concern. Organizations need to put together an action plan ensuring compliance with CSR precepts—in that the company's mission or organizational philosophy embodies a code of ethics and moral stance; while decision-making processes mirror the company's value systems, aiding in strategic planning.

Carrying this mission into the community, through a concerned partnership of education and philanthropy, elevates corporate stature, brand image, and customer loyalty. Complementing this aura of company pride are the outcomes of improved employee motivation, performance, and trust. Finally, profitability results from these positive activities, as clear accounting practices satisfy regulators and investors. Addressing environmental issues is a final piece of the puzzle, leading to a coherent overall strategy of CSR.

In looking at corporate social responsibility from a systems standpoint, it is of note that social, economic, and environmental reforms intertwine. Worldwide initiatives to advance standards of corporate conduct come to light in the 1999 *Global Sullivan Principles*, developed by the late Reverend Leon H. Sullivan. The objectives are:

To support economic, social, and political justice by companies where they do business;

To support human rights and to encourage equal opportunity at all levels of employment, including racial and gender diversity on decision-making committees and board;

To train and advance disadvantaged workers for technical, supervisory and management opportunities, and;

To assist with greater tolerance and understanding among peoples; thereby helping to improve the quality of life for communities, workers, and children with dignity and equality.

In summary, corporate social responsibility is a systematic program epitomizing organizational values and goals. Taking a strategic approach to integrating these values within a company's culture ensures stability. Encouraging an open forum of communication in setting ethical guidelines, clarifies performance criteria and enhances productivity. Asserting a message of quality and conscience to the community-at-large, solidifies an organization's commitment toward improving social, economic, and environmental welfare.

PART II

APPLYING AMERICAN BUSINESS VALUES
★★★

People have to feel needed. Frequently we just offer a job and 'perks.' We don't always offer people a purpose. When people feel there is a purpose and that they're needed, there's not much else to do except let them do the work.

Maya Angelou

Chapter Five

WORK and ACHIEVEMENT
★★★

Overview

The American emphasis on work and achievement can be traced to the early history of the Pilgrims and their beliefs in Puritanical ethics. Work was seen as a "calling" and way of life, planted in anti-hierarchical practices. To work hard, exhibit self-control, persevere, and plan ahead, were the roads to wealth and salvation.

Democracy in early America was geared toward self-government and education, with the idea that an open political and economic environment would unleash the talents and potentials of the people. The American philosophy was centered on "pragmatism" and adopting a flexible, innovative work culture. The place of government was to act as a nonrestricting, intervening entity in the preservation of freedom, and administration of a free market system.

The American frontier spirit that guided exploration and population movement throughout the United States, is the clearest illustration of a "collective individualism." It encompasses the values of creativity, risk taking, freedom of opportunity and open-mindedness. Trusting in human potential is the belief that imagination, discovery, and goal setting are constructive traits leading to a more enlightened result.

When the business organization of the future views itself on a mission of exploring new ways to get the job done, a sense of excitement and discovery drives the motivation of workers. When the management style reflects the leaders' perception that a team effort is imperative on any journey, the outcomes of satisfaction and productivity appear. Undertaking any expedition requires a knowledge and harmony with the outside environment, as well as a thorough understanding of the inner workings surrounding the explorers and their mission.

Capitalism and Personal Freedom
★★★

If growth is the primary goal of companies, then profit is a motive to reach this end. Making money sometimes reflects self-centered endeavors, and serves as an example of crass commercialism. The "bottom line," however, equates with businesses earning sufficient profits to grow, employ more people, and give back to the community. The lofty goals and values of a company rely on generating cash flow to support expansion.

The cornerstone of the free enterprise system, and even the personal freedom of everyone in America, is capitalism. This system is built on profit. To misunderstand these principles, or reject the intentions established by the Founders, is a neglect of "providing for the people by the people."

The core of capitalism also has an altruistic side. Many concerned companies are philanthropic in their contributions to society, and provide outstanding benefits to employees. Offering complete health care benefits, as well as profit sharing and retirement savings accounts to all workers, are staples of the profitable company. In addition, stakeholders representing investors, owners, and employees, gain increased value by receiving stock dividends, options, and matching programs. In today's world, big business really reflects the ownership of many small investors.

There has long been the debate over the ultimate goal of corporations. Is it merely to maximize shareholder value, or is there a value component to improve society. Whether this means being environmentally conscious or socially concerned, the company of tomorrow strikes a balance between profit, people and planet.

When "making money" equates with producing beneficial products and services; while bettering the lives of employees, and contributing to the global good; the words "profit" and "capitalism" take on new meanings. Whether helping the individual gain self-determination, or building bridges with the world, the free market system serves as the driving force toward growth and prosperity.

The All-American Success Story
★★★

America is the land of opportunity. This is the credo expounding the American dream of success, happiness, and a long-term outlook of fulfillment. From the country's early roots emphasizing hard work, there developed the truism that all people are created equal with the same chance of achievement.

There are so many rags to riches, mailroom to president stories; that these ideals are now an indelible part of the American spirit. Creating this sense of possibility is a norm worth highlighting in the American businesses world. Workers striving to do their best, with a focus on doing the best job possible, deserve special consideration and proper rewards. The worker guided by the organization's team goals, setting aside personal intent and credit, is the definitive employee.

The so-called port of entry for new employees within the forward-thinking organization serves as an open-ended gateway to prosperity. Quality employees appear throughout many departments of the productive organization. Launching and facilitating a career path takes place at any company level. It is important to recognize dedicated employees and move them promptly to positions of further responsibility and challenge.

People have different comfort levels and need for stimulation. The company in tune with employees' performance, attitudes, and striving for excellence, opens doors at the right time. Fostering a momentum, where employees move forward at a constant pace, boosts efficiency and creates a progressive work environment.

The Genius in All Americans
★★★

The idea that all individuals possess a special gift and unique perspective on the world, serves as a guideline to maximizing human potential. Some people label genius as being in the right place at the right time. This is a way of saying that when opportunity meets interest, the highest level of competence is possible.

The key to unlocking ideas is allowing individuals to define themselves and contribute to the decision-making process. Managers striving to uncover the underlying talents of workers create an employment climate encouraging innovation. It is obvious that the person doing the job on a daily basis has expert knowledge of the task, and its ramifications on other parts of the business. Therefore, soliciting ideas and suggestions from those "in the know," helps design new business strategies.

Showing a keen interest in employees from the time of hiring, and through orientation, creates an atmosphere of mutual respect. The process of recruiting and selecting employees often follows an unreliable, scientific line of reasoning. Utilizing overly-structured interview techniques, and analyzing biodata information for a perfect job match, constantly result in poor hiring decisions and employee turnover.

When companies evaluate prospective applicants in the qualitative areas of character, integrity, and potential for learning; an integrated, cohesive workforce develops. Given that individuals of high moral fiber adapt well and accept new challenges, organizations can fill many jobs with "gifted" individuals. This is a gift of open-mindedness, thirst for knowledge, and commitment to the overall goals of the organization.

The Independent Thinker
★★★

There is the misconception that encouraging independent thinking alienates the individual and fragments organizational goals. The paradox is that independent thinking actually deemphasizes self-interest, elevating group decision-making processes and improving performance. The concept of organizational efficiency reflects this notion—that collective individual efforts yield substantial outcomes.

When organizations empower workers to come up with new ideas and means of production as it benefits the whole, a powerful effect takes place merging the cumulative ideas of many. A wide spectrum of views and thoughts synthesize into a workable model of action. Finding common ground and exploring new ways of doing business within a group format, lead to ideas grounded in reason.

Poor decision making takes place in an organization or group when a "group think" mentality is supported. Fear of going against the grain, or voicing all possible scenarios, often yields a consensus based on the wants of management. Accommodating a full range of discourse simply opens all avenues of thought. Although this creative avenue may stray from the subject at hand or reach an unrelated tangent—in most cases, the right outcomes surface with future contingencies addressed.

"Thinking things through" is a difficult and elongated course of action when the organization confronts critical decision making. Easing this process by maximizing the independent thinking of diverse workers in varied departments, yields outcomes both comfortable and profitable.

Motivation Made Easy
★★★

Motivation conjures up the idea of action. Self-motivation and determination are actions firmly planted in all individuals. Working toward a goal or positive outcome is a drive prevalent among human beings. The drive to perform at a high level also supports the premise that goals themselves are not necessarily the dominant motivators. Individuals have a sense of pride and self-esteem, serving as a beacon for personal fulfillment.

Beyond the self-motivating theories, lies the framework of the individual being affected by intervening internal and external variables. When an organization supports and redirects the individual with a well-structured, complementary work environment, characterized by strong leadership, a win-win employee/employer relationship results.

People want treatment reflecting respect and equitable rewards for their contributions to the organization's objectives. It is human nature for workers to constantly monitor their own job performance (in terms of inputs/outcomes), and compare it to others in similar positions. True equitable treatment is in place when individuals feel justly rewarded for their efforts. This condition is a clue for managers to realize that linking pay to performance is pivotal, and the worker going the extra mile receives sufficient rewards.

Companies have the ability to influence positively the behavior of workers by establishing a clear set of policies and procedures, while allowing a degree of artistic freedom. Creating a path for employees to follow regarding performance, advancement, and quality of work, is a top priority of the progressive organization.

Providing for worker individuality, in concert with strategic management decision-making processes, establishes a business entity both dynamic and flexible. When companies appreciate individual employees, and understand what motivates them, a cohesive plan of mutual goals yields favorable results.

Personal Modeling and Integrity
★★★

Of all the values crucial to the success and achievement of an organization, integrity may be the most important. Companies categorize goodwill on their balance sheets and quantify this norm as a dynamic of productivity. The absolute significance of creating a high-minded, ethical employment climate cannot be overstated. The canon of a firm moral stature and nobility of purpose, coupled with business acumen, is the formula for gaining employee allegiance and attaining superior performance.

Integrity permeates all facets of an organization. Loyalty to a company's products, quality, and means of production equals loyalty to the company itself. A total commitment and pride of ownership in all corporate areas—manufacturing, distribution, research, finance, and marketing; motivates employees to think outside the box, delivering excellence.

When the owners and managers of the organization lead by example, a powerful structure is in place, encouraging participation by workers. Leadership behavior, and its effect on performance, has been studied and debated for years. From a simplistic point of view, individuals tend to emulate the personality and tone of their managers. This premise is a huge idea, given the potential to make a difference in the lives of people and their future.

The organization having a total focus on relating all company decisions and long-term planning to the core value of integrity, eliminates any doubts or distractions hindering growth. This so-called "soul of the company" is the intangible force of productivity.

Imagination and Originality
★★★

Doing things in new ways requires a high degree of sensitivity to what is taking place outside the organization, as well as comprehending the forces stimulating internal company functions. Imagination, experimentation, and curiosity are motivating factors to the company seeking operational proficiency.

Competition is a way of life in the American free enterprise system. The company embracing change, and filtering to its employees a risk-taking, open atmosphere of constructive criticism, prepares itself to compete and win in the new millennium.

Imagination and originality are often not the result of divine inspiration or a creative flash of brilliance. In countless cases, experimentation is the key component to discovering new modes. This exploration is hard work, amid the realization that perfection is not a realistic goal. At times, failure is the lightning rod for uncovering correct means of production. Having an open mind, and looking at the positive outcomes of any trial or endeavor, lead to the desired outcomes.

Accordingly, considering the opinions of all parties involved in a decision-making process casts the widest net on alternative problem-solving solutions. Allowing the broadest range of viewpoints stretches the boundaries of originality and creativity in seeking new ways of doing business. There is a constant internal conflict within organizations pitting order and constraint against innovation. When a company lets go and trusts its gut, a pragmatic and newfangled direction appears.

The Philanthropic Organization
★★★

From a system's outlook, organizations are not isolated entities, but part of a grand scale serving society and the well-being of humankind. This situation is a grand thesis to visualize and integrate within a company's mission and structure. Looking inward and outward simultaneously requires an almost selfless perspective on one's place in society. This great responsibility takes flight when actions and decisions favor a philosophy of giving.

By constantly looking at the full circle of employees, customers, community, and society-at-large; the progressive organization positively defines itself. The key is to rationalize the profit motive, distributing wealth in an egalitarian and equitable manner. Monetary achievement is the crowning asset for the corporation, and this outcome is the product of various forces.

Giving back in an unselfish way is a hallmark of the growth-oriented company. Reinvesting profits into new means of production, research, and development are constructive attitudes resulting in longevity for the company. Properly rewarding employees at all levels is the obvious way of ensuring security and meeting basic needs.

The questions of executive compensation and the maldistribution of profits, are current hotbeds of contention between companies and their stakeholders. The advanced corporation examines closely the way it conducts business relating to the standards of accountability, disclosure, and honesty. The ethics of equitably sharing wealth with employees, and favoring the outer community's welfare, serves as the heart of an organization's essence.

Summary
★★★

Work and achievement are basic characteristics of any organization or society. In order to devise a complete plan and view the big picture, companies consider a variety of interrelated factors—most specifically the career path of employees and atmosphere of learning.

The idea of a free enterprise system incorporates the large-scale platform for delivering a high standard of living and personal freedom to everyone. In going beyond materialistic wants, free markets embody trust, integrity, and respect for innovation. Opportunity is the keystone in an open society—raising the work ethic, and providing for a distribution of wealth beneficial to all.

Capitalism reflects a belief in the power of the individual to operate in a self-disciplined system. Self-government and independent thinking are ideologies specific to American democracy, helping unleash the talents and imagination of its members. The business world walks in tandem with these principles, offering an open forum free from heavy government restrictions and interference. Able corporations respect this environment, proving themselves as responsible and purposeful citizens.

The continuing success of American business follows the visions of entitlement, empowerment, and empathy. Opening a land of possibilities to skilled workers, while sharing the wealth at home and abroad, is a metaphor for doing business in the new millennium.

*A people that values its privileges above its
principles soon loses both.*

Dwight D. Eisenhower

Chapter Six

PRODUCTIVITY and EFFICIENCY
★★★

Overview

In the early twentieth century, Frederick Taylor formulated a theory of "scientific management," sparking an industrial efficiency movement occupied with time and motion studies. By applying a deterministic outlook to business operations, workers were assigned quotas, and job parts segmented into a precise division of labor.

A few years later, Elton Mayo's industrial psychology research into productivity yielded contrasting findings. At the Western Electric's Hawthorne factory in Chicago, it was incidentally discovered that the social interaction between researcher and worker was a key variable in increasing performance. Now commonly called the "Hawthorne Effect," Mayo concluded that people's work performance depends on both social issues and job content. There is a conflict of interest between manager's "logic of cost and efficiency," and worker's "logic of sentiment."

These findings started a debate on the decisive elements influencing industrial productivity, leading to new fields of study in organizational behavior. By the latter decades of the century, the emphasis on quantity of work was outpaced by research into quality management. The American social scientists, Joseph Juran and W. Edwards Deming, were early practitioners of "total quality management," having worked extensively in Japan after

World War Two. Juran was among the first to address human relations, and the "cultural resistance" of managers.

Deming also tackled the value component of quality, encouraging companies to adopt a management style favoring "transformational leadership." This is a posture of trust, cooperation, and empowerment. He espouses the philosophy that a firm's objectives favor the long term, with a "constancy of purpose" gearing toward customer satisfaction. Improvement is a goal closely aligning collective decision making and cross-functional communications between the departments of research, design, sales, and production. The innovative company is one able to coordinate its technical and human resource processes. In summing up his business philosophy, Deming states:

> It is important that an aim never be defined in terms of activity or methods. It must always relate directly to how life is better for everyone. The aim of the system must be clear to everyone in the system. The aim must include plans for the future. The aim is a value judgment.

Organizational Structure of Mutual Interests
★★★

Organizations tend to have detailed flow charts of hierarchical reporting relationships. Structure means a myriad of arrows connecting departments and divisions within the corporation. In reality, organizations are not tightly wound instruments, but loosely-coupled systems with slack and flexibility.

It is essential to have a well-delineated structure in place that mutually reflects the interests of owners, managers, and workers. This definition of structure goes beyond the traditional "top down" approach to management. Adopting a systematic structural arrangement helps route decision making in a continuous loop from manager to employee, and back. Opening lanes of communication throughout departments and divisions of a company creates an efficient and accurate flow of information.

Sound organizational structure allows a certain amount of autonomy and individual responsibility. While different parts and functions of a company will link, it is important to favor decentralization, forming separate operating divisions and subsidiaries. By establishing individual profit centers with their offices reporting to company headquarters, the organization is in balance, providing a value-rich environment conducive to enhanced productivity and quality.

Structure is a complicated subject matter, and often incorrectly seen as the sole outline for efficiency. The fine-tuned organization eliminates layers of middle management and enacts lateral reporting relationships. Simplifying structure is a company's goal, with the intent of instituting clear channels of communication—not mapping out positions of power.

The Suggestive Manager
★★★

Of all the components weaved within an organization's structure, one of the most commanding is the behavior of management. Setting a tone for the business in the areas of production, work rules, and goals is a sensitive topic, and one often receiving little consideration by profit-oriented institutions. Personality is a complex matter; deemed in management circles as difficult to change.

When an organization and its leaders manage human resources with a suggestive and congenial personality, workers reach a higher level of energy. Making employees satisfied and glad to be at work, heightens productivity and lessens tensions. Showing a genuine concern toward employees—emphasizing pride in the job done, soliciting differing opinions, and displaying common courtesy—builds a rock solid foundation.

The days of the hierarchical manager are gone. Naturally, there are basic ground rules inherent to any organization; but belittling employees or supervisors by intimidation are maxims evocative of past unproductive businesses. The initiatives of offering suggestions and establishing a two-way dialogue are non-threatening alternatives to solving problems. Fashioning a free atmosphere of generating ideas—expands workflow, satisfies customers, and enhances public relations.

Managers' insecurity with losing control or having competent subordinates take their job is a negative reaction damaging productivity in the long term. Managers welcoming employees' development and encouraging opportunities for promotion, receive one of management's greatest rewards—seeing employees grow and move forward.

Separating personal feelings and personality prejudices from the job at hand, are difficult but focal challenges to the organization of the future. Trusting employees, and letting go of the power that managers think is a perk, define the winners in the new millennium.

Trademarks and Company Conscience
★★★

The value-centered company of the next generation places extra emphasis on presenting a unified front reflecting quality and concern. The subject matter of trademarks goes beyond describing the distinctive characteristics of a product, service, or company. In today's business world, it is essential to have a "good name." Fairness and honesty are new symbols, going hand-in-hand with mantras such as "quality is job one."

Companies are looking toward establishing an in-depth "branding" campaign, that not only sells products, but serves as long-term program to "make ones mark" in the universe. Connecting with the customer is now a multi-level practice where companies demonstrate a caring spirit and positive identity. Creating an exemplary experience in selling products includes discerning the needs of the customer, and "over delivering" with top of the line service.

As advertising conveys messages beyond the scope of the product, a company "conscience" campaign with roots in ethical behavior, goes far in making a lasting impression with the consumer. When looking at organizations as entities with life-like qualities, the conscience or soul is the chief navigator. Charting a course locking on ethical actions and intentions, leads the organization to make decisions that improve society and the individual.

When the ultimate goal is to create a positive, virtuous experience, the image a company puts out into the world yields advantageous results. There should be a name association obvious to the public. The "what is" question asked about a company reflects not only the product, but also the company's commitment to improving social welfare.

Diversification, Innovation and Growth
★★★

The forward-thinking organization sees itself as a social scientist with microscope and telescope at hand. This does not mean predicting the future—it refers to examining the current state of affairs on a local, national and global level. Diversification is a function of companies aligning with changing social and cultural patterns.

"Change or be left behind" and "embrace change" are management sayings adorning many corporate offices. On the surface, these statements seem like simple proverbs. The crux of change management, however, relates to values of the company and society. "Change for change sake" will not solve problems, and often disrupts organizational efficiency. Any strategy of change relies on a detailed needs analysis and the long-term effect. Change can take place anytime—even when the organization is at the top of its game.

Openmindedness to the ideas and suggestions of employees is a starting point to perceiving the need for diversification and change. Coupling these insights with the cultural and material demands of society is the true definition of innovation. There has to be a fresh outlook and almost selfless approach to decision making.

Growth is the dominant goal of all organizations. When the company acts everyday as if it is just starting the business, an almost "organic" strategy develops, where today's seeds of new ideas yield tomorrows harvest of wealth. Corporations leaving behind old-school stubbornness and arrogance, take a "leap of faith" into realizing that organizations are open systems in constant change. "Everyday is a new day" best sums up the attitude of the innovative business model.

The Intangibles of Business Organization
★★★

Although America is a land of vast natural resources, the American genius for business organization and progress is increasingly a function of such intangibles as market analysis, sales training, advertising, and financial decentralization.

Understanding the customer, and how to position one's product, requires extensive and analytical research. Having a feel for the marketplace with an attention to current trends, is no longer an accurate means of predicting consumer behavior. It is pivotal that the organization undertakes statistical findings clarifying the existence of a strong market. Whether through structured interviews, focus groups, or demographic information—logic must prevail over feel. Giving customers what they really want is a simple but detailed task of asking the right questions.

The research, design, and development of a product or service are tasks that depend on a steady stream of information. From conception to distribution, all involved parties must understand the procedure. The final extension or sales force, responsible for placing the product into the marketplace, needs thorough knowledge of all production aspects. Eliciting feedback and continually updating field representatives to changes in production, yields a superior product.

Positioning a product or service in the marketplace is a process requiring repetition, emphasis, and emotion. After creating a need, it is imperative that the message reinforces the customer's wants by providing utility and satisfaction. It is virtually impossible to overexpose a product when it is presented in a thought-provoking, responsible, and caring context.

Adjunct to selling products, the intangibles of business organization also include the firm's general structural arrangements. Companies achieve stability when individual departments form—decentralizing and creating separate profit centers for the areas of production, marketing, research, operations, and distribution. This corporate design aids in constructing an innovative, independent, and ownership-based workplace. This climate acts as a springboard to the development and distribution of high-quality products and services.

Mastery of Understanding Society
★★★

As long as the world has existed, there has always been a need to study its people and understand their actions. Innovation suggests giving people what they really want. There is a constant exploring for new ways of doing things, and thinking outside the norm. Looking beyond material expansion and toward the maturation of ideas and thought processes, aids businesses in reaching an expanding world.

To "go with your best" is a motto portraying the American philosophy of true productivity. When a company brings to market the best products and services possible, a mastery of understanding society comes into focus. The ability to mirror the ideals of a society in one's business ventures is an enduring task and admirable goal.

Organizations often concentrate on the profit motive as an endpoint, without realizing that long-term performance is a function of intervening intangible variables. Determining the needs, wants, and aspirations of consumers in a complex marketplace, requires observation and testing of ideas. Being objective in establishing parameters for market research, data collection, and analysis goes beyond questionnaire design and statistics.

Successful product designers and sales forecasters adopt a normative course in finding the underlying motives and cultural forces behind consumer behavior. Usually, this means conducting lengthy interviewing sessions, and outlining probing questions. Old-fashioned, structured research based simply on open or close-ended questions only scratches the surface. Additionally, large samples of data with little depth offer short-term fixes.

The organization striving for a long-term commitment with the consumer, designs robust, detailed surveys with an emotional content; bringing a high degree of clarity. A few thought-provoking, action-packed surveys trump a large sample every time. These comprehensive, individual interviews also complement the focus group method; in that group settings often elicit similar opinions among members when random participants are brought together to evaluate products. By choosing a diverse group of individuals, and "going deep" with their true feelings, the organization gains the accurate information necessary to set long-term plans, policies, and products.

Exporting Corporate Culture
★★★

Getting one's message out into the world originates from a corporate affairs' department in charge of projecting a unified strategy. Companies need to realize that culture is the center of their industrial universe. By assembling a team, with the task to formulate, coordinate, and implement all company policies across operational areas, a clear-cut message, method, and image is in place, ready for launching.

The ability to "cookie cut" or take a successful business operation into different neighborhoods around the globe depends on stability and consistency in operations. Although there is the obvious situation where local customs dictate certain business activities, the base or underlying value systems of the company are the attraction to expansion and success. Cultural norms vary in different parts of the world, and the exporting of American culture serves as a complimentary resource to the local community.

Whereas customs may change from one civilization to another, people everywhere have a common bond and viewpoint toward what is right. American value systems may represent conventions different from other countries, but the message is the same—quality of life is the ultimate goal.

Organizations adhering to the attitude of "people first," do well in exporting their ideas. Trying to define the soul of an organization follows a detailed road of discovery; similar to the archaeologist digging for clues to history. Putting the pieces of this puzzle together takes considerable searching and testing to produce a uniform statement of purpose.

Summary
★★★

Productivity and efficiency take on new meanings as technologically advanced societies compete globally for the consumer dollar. Economists still measure productivity by gross domestic product and output-per-worker, but these figures mean little if product quality lags, and the mix is inappropriate to the buyer.

Getting in-sync with the realities of a changing marketplace filled with over choice but little differentiation, are tasks confronting the twenty-first-century business. Organizations have taken a short-term outlook on producing goods, with little reference to company goals and values. Without formulating a flexible organizational structure and management style, the business entity becomes rigid, lacking style and substance.

Eliminating waste by taking risks is an attitude somewhat incongruent with executive decision making. This approach does not mean out-of-the-blue operational and marketing strategies. It refers to doing your homework, and trusting your instincts if the data diverges from common marketplace knowledge.

Efficiency closely aligns with the idea of synergy—where the whole is greater than the sum of the parts. Companies are looking for ways to streamline operations and get more with less. Engaging the opinions of workers at all levels, and encouraging solutions to productivity gains, are fundamental to understanding efficiency. Managing workers with sensitivity to their opinions and performance is a difficult exercise. It is necessary to have a company-wide value system in place, supporting goals of the organization and workers' satisfaction.

Perhaps the most difficult concept to grasp is the idea that a company's products and services mirror the values of society. These "wants" of the consumer reflect both utility and emotion. In today's world, business organizations do not only stand for quality. They exemplify "quality of life."

Chapter Seven

UNITY and PATRIOTISM
★★★

Overview

When Americans think of Unity and Patriotism, they gravitate to the values of a free and democratic society. This feeling signifies admiration for the customs and traditions of a government and society promoting positive civic virtues.

The attachment to a community or country is a natural and universal attitude. Having a sense of identification within a group is a needed requirement in helping shape the healthy person. Accepting membership into the customs and beliefs of an organization supports the principles of belonging and allegiance.

Within the American democracy, the people share a willingness to serve, and are expected to obey the laws. It is the individual's responsibility to have information of the laws, and knowledge regarding current affairs. Freedom of expression and access to information are embedded statutes.

It is important to appreciate patriotism as a unique form of loyalty and devotion. This concept is a clear departure from the overzealous, exaggerated behaviors characterizing certain tyrannical groups. Americans covet their independence, and open society of ideas.

Although Americans value a separation of work and family life, the progressive business organization sees the need for offering a complete, integrated work experience—

one giving workers meaning in their jobs, and a sense of family.

Focusing on the individual's rights in a free society; while looking outward to our family of nations, and extending an olive branch, is the creed of America's mission toward peace and fellowship.

The True Meaning of Happiness
★★★

What is happiness? Is it strictly an internal good feeling, or is it a by-product of complex factors influencing an individual? True happiness is a state of mind achieved when someone meshes with the environment. When a person is appreciated as an individual, with a specific role in a group or organization, enlightenment is attained.

To understand the uniqueness of each individual is a daunting task. People bring a history of needs, wants, and aspirations into the workplace. Discovering the underlying talents of workers requires a certain degree of empathy, listening, and open-mindedness by business leaders. Defining a role leading to optimum performance and satisfaction is a matter of matching job requirements with the individual's background and skill set.

Conventional business wisdom states that employees should form a precise match with job descriptions. This outlook is partly true, but the highly evolved organization knows that talent comes first, and workers deserve the opportunity to define themselves within the context of the job.

Companies can aid the worker's identity within the organization by providing effective leadership and group practices. This includes designing jobs that offer interaction, variety, significance, and responsibility. Instituting a supportive management structure and feedback mechanism, enabling the individual to receive and evaluate information about performance standards, are springboards to job satisfaction.

The Components of Creating a Positive Attitude
★★★

The forward-moving company orchestrates a climate that has order and direction. Organization is in place, insuring a smooth transition of ideals across all levels of the business. Efficiency breeds effectiveness. This relationship is the keystone of any enterprise.

How do order and efficiency relate to creating a positive attitude? It is necessary to have a solid framework in place to instill confidence. When this baseline is inherent in an organization, the components of belonging, pride, and devotion are nurtured. By forging a consistent tone of trust and order, the enterprise is ready to provide a business culture suitable to the employee.

Building a sense of identification and ownership of goals between a company and its employees are ongoing processes. Employers must prove themselves to employees. It is a natural tendency to expect workers to serve the company, however, the fully functioning organization sees through this, realizing that the company itself is the positive force to forming an efficient and tightly knit operation. Meeting each other "halfway" is a fair illustration of the innate employment contract between employee and employer.

Equitable treatment is evident when the organization pursues a structure based on egalitarian practices in hiring, reward systems, performance appraisal, and accountability. The stance of the management team sets the stage as a role model for the acceptable and desirable behaviors of employees.

Participative Management for Everyone
★★★

In the new millennium, an overhaul of management attitudes and policies is taking place. In today's world, workers have a greater depth of life experiences, talents, and education. No longer can companies view individuals as a function, or source of capital. The twenty-first-century worker deserves respect and compassion befitting a valuable human resource. To solicit input and ideas from employees at all organizational levels, fashions an open arena of opinions.

Resistance to change is the biggest obstacle in employing a participative management structure. Inflexible rule is a common theme throughout the American business community. This arrangement is not an accurate portrayal of what Americans want, nor is it reflective of the country's democratic heritage. Of course, the owners of business hold all the cards, but in loosening their grip and entrusting workers, satisfaction rules.

In applying a structure where all echelons of an organization are open to new ideas, constructive criticism, and simple dialogue—efficiency increases, heightening productivity. Respect for other's ideas is an integral part of any relationship, and the business world is no different.

Group decision making is a powerful tool available to all departments of the organization. Establishing an open platform for the exchange, recommendation, and appraisal of ideas, aids in developing outstanding business standards and procedures. When a consensus forms, relating to the change or design of any operational issue, action quickly turns into implementation.

Loyalty, Nobility and Brotherhood
★★★

The best way for an organization to gain loyalty from its employees is to embrace the values of American culture. Because these values are ingrained in the American psyche, practicing these ideals creates an environment favorable to mutual trust.

Trust is the prerequisite to higher degrees of organizational unity. Gaining commitments to the causes and mission of a company are the building blocks to solidifying a community of workers.

A true brotherhood of workers exemplifies the honorable traits of loyalty and nobility. Establishing an esprit de corps affirms a faith in character and integrity. In earning the trust of employees through open communications and respect, a devotion to the company develops. This rapport is especially important in times of organizational change or crisis. Attaining the pledge of employee allegiance by projecting an atmosphere of truth and decorum, helps prepare the organization for future opportunities and challenges.

The advanced enterprise understands that originating new ways of doing business, and providing exemplary service, are details closely aligned with stability. When a company retains employees and advances its history with a strong nucleus of workers, a partnership of ideas, convictions, and performance standards is in place—resulting in a powerful business entity capable of advanced thinking and increased productivity.

Employment Climate and Culture
★★★

The overall working conditions within a company or enterprise define its commitment to workers, and potential for opportunity. Delivering an experience of fulfillment and security is the admirable career path that employees expect, and attentive employers strive to develop. Managers at all levels of an organization best serve their workers' goals in creating a climate of open interaction and humility.

The approachable manager brims with humor, shows concern for the well-being of employees, and projects a "can do" attitude. An atmosphere of fun, creativity, and flexibility gives an organization leverage in adapting to change and maximizing the productivity of workers.

There is an exchange-relationship taking place in all organizations. When a company sells itself to employees, a reciprocal relationship transpires, wherein the worker buys into the company's ownership. When this mutual interest occurs, the company is ready and capable of outreaching into society and forming a truly holistic organization.

Culture is the distinctive identity of an organization. It is the creative stamp reflecting the company's desire to make a difference in the lives of its employees and the community at large. Organizational culture depicts the total package of beliefs and attitudes entrenched in the core of the company's mission—operational efficiency, ethical conduct, and equitable treatment for all.

Training in the New Millennium
★★★

Knowledge is the essential component of any institution looking to formulate a cohesive environment geared toward performance. Training is an investment that is sometimes difficult to quantify in terms of immediate results. Companies have been shortsighted in realizing the long-term impact of designing effective learning strategies. Training is a process analogous to planting seeds for the future harvest.

A communal approach to instituting training, centers on involving all organizational levels and operational areas. The forceful and longest lasting training programs are those seeking input from all participants—prior to, during, and after delivery. There is a constant assessment and refinement of programs to address changing working conditions and goals.

When the company approaches training in a systematic fashion, not isolating this activity to certain groups or job descriptions, a fluid means of production is the outcome. This refers to the idea that workers are aware of, and potentially involved, with training agendas taking place at other levels and departments of the organization. By monitoring interdepartmental training programs for consistency, a comprehensive itinerary comes forth, destined to succeed.

Training is a benefit to the individual. It represents a setting for employees to act as facilitators and team leaders. It is an arena for group interaction, as well as a forum to exchange ideas and learn about co-workers' backgrounds. From a pure human resources point of view, training provides the organization with an opportunity to eliminate any discrimination, while broadcasting a message of learning, cooperation, and achievement.

Organizational Mission and Family Values
★★★

When formulating a company or organization, the key premises are the adoption of a mission statement, organizational structure, and value system. These core building blocks epitomize a company's justification for existence, model for acceptance by members, and road map for future expansion. These bases are subject to reformulation, modification, or change at any time, when the goals are advantageous to the members.

When the mission is clearly stated, and relates to outcomes and goals, the members of the organization develop a collective consciousness. When questions of policy or change confront the organization, an examination of the mission statement helps solve problems, and offers logical solutions.

Looking at an organization as a family is the easiest way to develop a plan for success. Making friends is the simple task innate to establishing a community built on character. Showing interest, being courteous, keeping promises, saying 'thank you'—these are the central characteristics of the "natural" organization.

Robert W. Woodruff, former President of The Coca-Cola Company, who built the company into the model for American business in the twentieth century, liked to say:

> The five most important words in dealing with people are 'I am proud of you.' The four most important words are 'what is your opinion?' The three most important words are 'if you please.' The two most important words are 'thank you.' The least important word is 'I'.

Internalizing the mission of developing valued employees is the ultimate statement a company can make. The principle is that every job is the most important. The employee who unselfishly strives to do the best job will be recognized and rewarded. These rewards are those of pride, belonging, and a sense of community. These are the determinants of advanced productivity, profit, and progress.

Summary
★★★

The core values of Unity and Patriotism symbolize the glue of the organization. Creating a unified entity that thinks and acts in harmony depends upon managing many variables. The thorough integration of workers with the company's mission, and the extension of this mission into the community of both customers and neighbors, secures the organization's long-term survival. When a shared feeling and appreciation of what the company stands for—in its products, means of production, distribution, and follow-through service is evident, prosperity is the result.

Engaging the opinions of workers regarding new ideas and improved means of production, opens innovative ways of doing business, resulting in a more efficient operation. Empowering workers at all levels with responsibility and team-leadership capabilities, helps break down barriers hindering productivity by exposing creative solutions. Companies add value to jobs through complete training and development programs, upgrading the compensable factors of skill and responsibility.

Adopting a consultative stance to decision making allows the organization to cover all bases relating to performance—ensuring an action plan with roots in reason and accountability. Developing effective, consensual decision-making processes are goals attainable by the company fostering trust, communication, and a climate of respect for individuals' ideas.

When an organization implements this arena of collective thinking, a loyalty to the company's values, ideals, and mission becomes apparent. Gaining the commitment of workers is a constant process—part of a reciprocal relationship embedded in understanding the hearts and minds of a community of people

We live in a time of transition, an uneasy era which is likely to endure for the rest of the century. During this period we may be tempted to abandon some of the time-honored principles and commitments which have been proven during the difficult times of past generations. We must never yield to this temptation. Our American values are not luxuries, but necessities—not the salt in our bread, but the bread itself.

Jimmy Carter

Chapter Eight

CONCLUSIONS
★★★

A *Declaration of American Business Values* outlines a course of action and conceptual model for organizational change—directing companies to approach the task of designing and applying value systems with a strong will and resolve. Addressing ethical platforms, and integrating them into the work culture, requires wisdom, conviction, and a sense of purpose.

The philosophy and mission of a company express and represent a flexible format of work rules based on agreed-upon values. This multidimensional model of productivity enforces the qualitative values of ethics, equity, and efficiency. Relating these norms to the individual, organization, and society, formulates a matrix of possibilities and challenges.

Companies have the ability to influence positively the lives of employees. This premise is a huge responsibility and opportunity for transformational learning and career advancement. By providing an honest wage package, and opening possibilities for self-determination on the job, the firm of the future goes a long way in maximizing employee performance and stimulating personal growth.

Adopting a family-first mentality is the easiest way to start the activity of building a value-based organization. Forming a cooperative unit of workers and managers aligning with a society of stakeholders, paints a clear picture of the organization's identity. Simplifying reporting relationships and creating channels of communication are necessary structural arrangements. Breaking down positions of power, and creating an egalitarian climate, invigorates participation, resulting in a high degree of trust. Upper level management personnel need to "walk the shop floor" regularly, and encourage suggestions from all departments and levels of the company.

Additionally, showing concern for the welfare of employees goes beyond on-the-job performance. John Wooden, the legendary college basketball coach talks about bringing out the best in people:

> People want to believe you are sincerely interested in them as a person, not just for what they can do for you. . . . In the workplace, you'll get better cooperation and results if you are sincerely interested in people's families and interests, not simply how they do their job. This will bring productive results. Most people try to live up to expectations. It always comes back to courtesy, politeness and consideration.

Recent research studies confirm the need for open and honest communications on the job. The Randstad *2006 Employee Review* survey reveals disparities in how employers and employees view the employment relationship. For example, 72 percent of employers say fostering employee development is important, whereas only 49 percent of employees say management is adhering to this practice. In addition, 86 percent of employees cite "feeling valued" as the most important factor for happiness on the job, while only 47 percent of employers say it exists. The report summarizes:

> Like water beginning to boil, the bubbles are starting to form and there soon could be a full movement of workers toward companies that offer the components employees rate highest on their most-wanted list: better pay and development opportunities, someplace

where leadership walks the talk and a workplace where employees feel valued.

American Democracy was founded on the principles of giving its citizens a meaningful, orderly life guided by sensible leadership. Democracy only takes hold if the participants are able to act on, and form the principles of governance. The business world applies these ideals by providing workers with significant job experiences, and opportunities for input, supported by concerned leadership.

The concept of freedom represents individual decision making aided by a structured environment. This principle is a common sense doctrine favoring shared rule setting as a creation "of the people, by the people, and for the people."

Within the free market economy, a so-called "manifest destiny" is inherent, allowing members to chart their own course. Individualism highlights an approach to clarifying roles and influencing productive behaviors. The mitigating functions of leadership, structure, and job content are all variables under the control of organizations. Putting together a work environment conducive to advanced performance, points to comprehending the bases of human motivation, and imparting equitable rewards.

Caring companies assume the responsibility of being global citizens, and enforcing ethical standards, in an atmosphere of concern for the individual and society. Being able to bring the intangible aspect of morality into the workplace, requires a socialization process extending across the personnel functions of recruiting, selection, orientation, and training. Corporate social responsibility is the goal of all organizations—from entrepreneurial start-up firms to multinational corporations.

The values of work and achievement further the need for continuing education and career development programs.

Managers should encourage these activities and enforce this commitment to new learning and experimentation.

Regarding productivity and efficiency, organizations need to flatten hierarchical reporting relationships and streamline operations. Obtaining accurate research methodology is a by-product of open dialogue between workers, managers, and consumers. Taking a holistic approach to comprehending the sphere of influence on the company goes a long way in molding the "stamp" of the organization. The democratic business entity defines itself with a unique personality and image, where compassion and quality rule conduct. Establishing a distinct "brand" reflecting the organization's mission, positions the company for future opportunities.

The firm inspiring a sense of community and unity, stations itself for long-term success and the retention of employees. Pride in ownership is the mantra of a family of workers. In the twenty-first century, a new definition of efficiency reflects not only social responsibility, but also the proper utilization of human resources. Strategic planning in research, marketing, quality control, and new product development are goals equal in importance to productivity and performance.

Bringing a democratic culture into the work environment is an ongoing course of action, similar to instituting a democratic government in a foreign country. Integrating ideas, principles, and values in a new community follows a step-wise progression, where individuals buy into the program one at a time. This "diffusion" is similar in nature to the process of instituting change or innovation.

In seeking to take the concepts of employee ownership, trust, and commitment to the highest level, organizations face the critical issues of our time—foremost, the implementation of fair pay practices. The topic of excessive executive compensation is a sensitive topic with workers, and in stark contrast to those seeking a "living wage." Sharing the wealth describes the progressive company.

On a national level, the proposed Fair Pay Act of 2005 signifies the latest, in a series of concerted efforts, toward bringing equal pay for equal work legislation to the forefront. One of the prime moving forces in bringing pay equity to practice will be a deeper examination and validation of job evaluation procedures.

As the State of Oregon's job evaluation plan brought to light, there is a perceived discrepancy between objective standards of job evaluation, and the subjective wants of executive decision makers—especially in relation to hiring external management consultants and designing plans. From an ideal and value-centered perspective, job evaluation prepared internally by a company's human resources department is the best solution.

Although Oregon's job evaluation program was seen to be problematic in implementation; staying the course and realizing that social welfare change is a developing process, define the attitudes of pay equity advocates. Major strides have been made over the years, and future efforts will learn from these studies. The fact that wages have increased and workers feel involved, gives credence to the continued use of job evaluation as an effective tool in eliminating wage discrimination.

This outlook reinforces the need for an improved formula to educate organizations on the subject of pay equity. From a broad scholastic viewpoint, the subject matter of job analysis has received minimum attention within academic institutions. With the exception of basic management courses in compensation administration, there has been an absence of functional class work pertaining to job evaluation. It is advisable that certification programs be part of the curriculum at the Community College level and beyond.

Developing an interdisciplinary degree program; covering course work in the fields of management, psychology, sociology, statistics, and computer science; addresses specific job evaluation areas ranging from questionnaire design to factor analysis. The time has come for pay equity to move to the top of business management studies, as it clearly influences employee motivation and productivity.

The future of job evaluation concentrates on standardizing job worth criteria across divergent industries and job classifications. Presently, jobs are compared for equal value—usually those performed by men and women. For example, the State of Minnesota compared the wage rates of male senior corrections officers and female registered nurses for equity. This procedure has been a staple for comparable worth supporters. The public sector has taken the lead, with voluntary compliance by private firms the next step in solidifying pay equity.

As pay equity research and implementation methods advance, a universal paradigm of job worth evolves—based primarily on a "value score" reflecting the factors of effort, skill, responsibility and working conditions. Determining wage rates requires an in-depth analysis of many gradations relating to these factors, constructed by expert job analysts with input from workers and managers. After determining a score, the results bind to the external labor market, serving as a baseline for upgrading salaries.

Additionally, educational initiatives set by the EEOC and other concerned parties, such as the National Committee on Pay Equity, help companies define and implement a workable pay equity plan. This premise of disclosure is especially crucial to employees who measure and compare job inputs and outcomes to others, as predicated by equity theory of motivation, resulting in satisfaction.

The proper defining and weighting of compensable factors is a complex procedure for job evaluation practitioners, and still in its infancy. There has been an omission of value-related factors, and lack of breadth in calculating job worth. There are several content providers currently offering job evaluation software and solutions, utilizing different methods of delivery. Management consulting firms have proprietary systems, able to tailor a package to the specific needs of companies. The use of multivariate analysis is a powerful tool for the job analyst, and one requiring a sharp eye on social and technical factors.

Once pay equity is in place, progressive companies monitor the results and account for cost-of-living increases and merit plans. Organizations need to complement salaries with incentive-based compensation programs. Motivational theories substantiate the pay for performance link, enforcing the premise that individual and group rewards are catalysts for company growth.

The topic of setting wages is a subject matter that economists have been debating for years. From a counterpoint of view, the thesis dictates that rising wages will trigger inflation and higher interest rates, slowing the economy. This perception is also a point of contention on a global scale. Although certain sectors such as manufacturing are susceptible to downturns, there is a folly to this reasoning, as full employment and pay satisfaction conclusively result in higher company revenues, earnings, and quality.

The major pitfall facing executive decision makers is the notion that bottom line profitability necessitates eliminating workers and cutting expenses. Providing exemplary customer service is the driving force within our service economy, and future business leaders will have to make this a top priority.

In *The Turning Point,* author Fritjof Capra gives a global view of economic theory:

> The evasion of value-related issues has led economists to retreat to easier but less relevant problems, and to disguise value conflicts by using elaborate technical language. The trend is particularly strong in the United States, where there is now a widespread belief that all problems—economic, political, or social—have technical solutions.

In the new millennium, American business prosperity will be contingent on paying close attention to the interdependence of America's value systems. Finding value-related solutions, apart from technical answers, will help normalize business relations, divert worker alienation, and foster a collective corporate culture.

The achieving business organization of the future will look inward, examine its cultural history, and provide a value system mirroring the best of America—creating a workplace based on idealism and reality.

Daniel Webster once wrote:

> Let us develop the resources of our land, build up its interests and see whether we also, in our day and generation, may perform something worthy to be remembered.

The key American resources of the future will be our value systems, and the ability to refine and reflect on our culture and heritage. Assimilating these values into our business communities will be the keystone to establishing a secure foundation for all Americans.

A Declaration of American Business Values shines a light on the perspective that individual values are not standalone items. Instead, values relate to one another forming a systems relationship. Productivity is an outcome closely tied to equity, social responsibility, and concern for the individual. Companies taking a "leap of faith" in entrusting and empowering employees will win big. Although the corporate owners of capital may be reluctant to share what they started, it is tantamount that mutually beneficial goals and rewards are on the table. Risk taking is an endeavor concerning not only operational matters, but a belief in the workers of production.

America's inventive mind will produce breakthrough advances in numerous fields. The new millennium will show great progress in the medical sciences of bioengineering and nanotechnology. Computer parallel processing and high-speed connectivity will dominate communications. Robotic factories will revolutionize machinery and manufacturing sectors. Automobiles will run on hydrogen fuel cells, supporting a global stance on ecological concerns. Space exploration will uncover new mysteries of the universe and create laboratories in the sky. Technology will command the landscape. The focal point in extending and stabilizing innovation, will be the close attention to our human resources.

The ability to manage employees, provide substantial work experiences, and establish fair labor practices, will determine the sustainability of economic expansion. When American business can examine the big picture, acting as responsible community-driven citizens, an energizing force will envelop the organization, driving new levels of worker satisfaction and productivity.

The twenty-first century will be an era of human potential. The keys to unlocking new ways of doing business—in developing new products, advancing technological solutions, and extending the quality of life—will be in motivating the American worker. Understanding the behaviors and goals of a population, points to examining the cultural value systems, and incorporating those ideals into business principles of organization. As a civilization progresses, forging new ideas of self-expression and growth, the crux to sustainability is harmony among members with an emphasis toward the common good.

The American democracy, founded on freedom and equality, is the most advanced form of government in the world. It is still evolving as a quality way of life for all members. Given political unrest around the world, Americans are looking inward and appreciating the United States spirit of opportunity and prosperity. In the new millennium, democratic commandments will extend deeper into the livelihood of its citizens, beyond the home life, and into the workplace.

When American business practitioners can take the core value components inherent in our Constitution, and make a workable model of economic development, a true equality will empower the individual, organization, and community.

The measure of the restoration lies in the extent to which we apply social values more noble than mere monetary profits.

Franklin D. Roosevelt

BIBLIOGRAPHY
★★★

Books

Acker, J. *Doing Comparable Worth: Gender, Class, and Pay Equity.* Philadelphia: Temple University Press, 1989.

Almond, G.A., and Verba, S. *The Civic Culture.* Princeton, NJ: Princeton University Press, 1963.

Andrews, K.R. *The Concept of Corporate Strategy.* New York: Richard D. Irwin, 1987.

Argyris, C. *Integrating the Individual and the Organization.* New York: John Wiley and Sons, 1964.

Barrett, D.N. *Values in America.* Notre Dame, IN: University of Notre Dame Press, 1961.

Belcher, D.W. *Compensation Administration.* Englewood Cliffs, NJ: Prentice-Hall, 1974.

Blow, M. (ed.) *The American Heritage History of the Thirteen Colonies.* New York: American Heritage Publishing Co., 1967

Bowen, C.D. *Miracle at Philadelphia: The Story of the Constitutional Convention May to September 1787.* Boston: Little, Brown and Co., 1966.

Brunner, E., and Hallenbeck, W.C. *American Society: Urban and Rural Patterns.* New York: Harper and Brothers, 1955.

Candler, C.H. *Asa Griggs Candler.* Atlanta: Foote and Davies, 1950.

Capra, F. *The Turning Point.* New York: Simon and Schuster, 1982.

Cavanagh, G.F. *American Business Values* (3rd ed.). Englewood Cliffs, NJ: Prentice-Hall, 1990.

Cohen, H. (ed.) *The American Culture.* Boston: Houghton Mifflin, 1968.

Cowell, F.R. *Values in Human Society.* Library of Congress: F. Porter Sargent, 1970.

Crosby, P.B. *Quality is Free: The Art of Making Quality Certain.* New York: McGraw-Hill, 1979.

Curti, M. *The Growth of American Thought.* New York: Marper and Brothers, 1943.

Cyert, R.M., and March, J.G. *A Behavioral Theory of the Firm.* Englewood Cliffs, NJ: Prentice Hall, 1963.

Deci, E.L. *Intrinsic Motivation: Theory and Research.* New York: Plenum Publishing, 1975.

DeFleur, M.L., D'Antonio, W.V., and DeFleur, L.B. *Sociology: Man in Society.* Glenview, IL: Scott, Foresman, 1971.

Deming, W.E. *Out of Crisis.* Cambridge, MA: MIT Press, 1986.

Dobyns, L., and Crawford-Mason, C. *Quality or Else: The Revolution in World Business.* Boston: Houghton Mifflin, 1991.

Dubin, R. (ed.) *Handbook of Work, Organization and Society.* Chicago: Rand-McNally, 1976.

Evans, S.M., and Nelson, B.J. *Wage Justice, Comparable Worth and the Paradox of Technocratic Reform.* Chicago: University of Chicago Press, 1989.

Festinger, L.A. *A Theory of Cognitive Dissonance.* Stanford, CA: Stanford University Press, 1957.

Freeman, R.E., and Gilbert, D.E.,Jr. *Corporate Strategy and the Search for Ethics.* Englewood Cliffs, NJ: Prentice Hall, 1988.

Friedman, M. *Capitalism and Freedom.* Chicago: The University of Chicago Press, 1962.

Gabriel, R.H. *American Values: Continuity and Change.* Westport, CT: Greenwood Press, 1974.

Glueck, W.F. *Personnel: A Diagnostic Approach* (2nd ed.). Dallas, TX: BPI, 1978.

Goodell, E. (ed.) *Social Venture Network: Standards of Corporate Social Responsibility.* San Francisco: Social Venture Network, 1999.

Graham, S. *American Culture.* New York: Harper and Brothers, 1957.

Gross, B. *A Great Society?* New York: Basic Books, 1968.

Hague, J.A. (ed.) *American Character and Culture.* Deland, FL: Everett Edwards Press, 1964.

Henderson, R.I. *Compensation Management: Rewarding Performance* (3rd ed.). Reston, VA: Reston Publishing Co., 1982.

Hersey, P., and Blanchard, K.H. *Management of Organizational Behavior: Utilizing Human Resources.* (3rd ed.). Englewood Cliffs, NJ: Prentice-Hall, 1977.

Herzberg, F. *Work and the Nature of Man.* Cleveland: World Publishing, 1966.

Herzberg, F., Mausner, B., and Synderman, B. *The Motivation to Work* (2nd ed.). New York: John Wiley and Sons, 1959.

Homans, G.C. *Social Behavior: Its Elementary Forms.* New York: Harcourt, Brace, and World, 1961.

Ivancevich, J.M., and Matteson, M.T. *Stress and Work: A Managerial Perspective.* Glenview, IL: Scott, Foresman, 1980.

Jaques, E. *Equitable Payment.* New York: John Wiley and Sons, 1961.

Jarvis, P. *Adult and Continuing Education: Theory and Practice* (2nd ed.). New York: Routledge, 1995.

Juran, J. *Managerial Breakthrough.* New York: McGraw-Hill, 1964.

Kahn, E.J. *The Big Drink.* New York: Random House, 1960.

Kardines, A. *The Individual and His Society.* New York: Alfred A. Knopf, 1955.

Katz, D., and Kahn, R.L. *The Social Psychology of Organizations* (2nd ed.). New York: John Wiley and Sons, 1978.

Korman, A.K. *The Psychology of Motivation.* Englewood Cliffs, NJ: Prentice-Hall, 1974.

Kroeber, A.L. *The Nature of Culture.* Chicago: The University of Chicago Press, 1952.

Laski, H.J. *The American Democracy.* New York: Viking Press, 1948.

Lawler, E.E. *Pay and Organizational Effectiveness: A Psychological View.* New York: McGraw-Hill, 1971.

Lawler, E.E. *Motivation in Work Organizations.* Belmont, CA: Brooks/Cole Publishing, 1973.

Lewin, K. *Field Theory in Social Science.* New York: Harper and Row, 1951.

Linton, R. *The Tree of Culture.* New York: Alfred A. Knopf, 1955.

Lipset, S.M. *The First New Nation.* New York: Basic Books, 1963.

March, J.G., and Simon, H.A. *Organizations.* New York: John Wiley and Sons, 1958.

Maslow, A.H. *Motivation and Personality.* New York: Harper and Row, 1954.

Maslow, A.H. *Eupsychian Management.* Homewood, IL: Richard D. Irwin, 1965.

Mayo, E. *The Human Problems of an Industrial Civilization.* New York: The Macmillan Co., 1933.

McClelland, D.C. *The Achieving Society.* New York: Van Nostrand, 1961.

McGregor, D. *The Human Side of Enterprise.* New York: McGraw-Hill, 1960.

Merriam, S.B., and Cunningham, P.M. (eds.) *Handbook of Adult and Continuing Education.* San Francisco: Jossey-Bass, 1989.

Mezirow, J. *Transformative Dimensions of Adult Learning.* San Francisco: Jossey-Bass, 1991.

Michener, J.A. *This Noble Land.* New York: Ballantine Publishing, 1996.

Miller, P. *The American Puritans.* Garden City, NY: Doubleday, 1956.

Myrdal, G. *An American Dilemma.* New York: Harper and Brothers, 1944.

Nadler, D.A., Hackman, J.R., and Lawler, E.E. *Managing Organizational Behavior.* Boston: Little, Brown and Co., 1979.

Ormrod, J.E. *Human Learning* (2nd ed.). Englewood Cliffs, NJ: Prentice Hall, 1995.

Parkes, H.B. *The American Experience.* New York: Alfred A. Knopf, 1955.

Parrington, V.L. *Major Currents in American Thought* (book III). New York: Harcourt Brace and Company, 1930.

Parsons, T. *The Social System.* New York: Free Press, 1951.

Pastin, M. *The Hard Problems of Management: Gaining the Ethics Edge.* San Francisco: Jossey-Bass, 1986.

Peters, J.M., and Jarvis, P. *Adult Education: Evolution and Achievements in a Developing Field of Study.* San Francisco: Jossey-Bass, 1991.

Porter, L.W., and Lawler, E.E. *Managerial Attitudes and Performance.* Homewood, IL: Irwin-Dorsey, 1968.

Potter, D.M. *People of Plenty.* Chicago: The University of Chicago Press, 1954.

Reynolds, L.T., Larr, T., and Henslin, J.W. *American Society.* New York: David McKay Co., 1973.

Rogers, C. *A Way of Being.* Boston: Houghton Mifflin Co., 1980.

Rokeach, M. *Beliefs, Attitudes, and Values: A Theory of Organization and Change.* San Francisco: Jossey-Bass, 1968.

Sovereign, K.L. *Personnel Law.* Reston, VA: Reston Publishing Co., 1984.

Sumner, W.G. *Folkways.* New York: The New American Library, 1960 (originally published in 1906).

Sutton, F.X., Harris, S.E., Kaysen, C., and Tobin, J. *The American Business Creed.* Cambridge, MA: Harvard University Press, 1956.

Taylor, F.W. *The Principles of Scientific Management.* New York: Harper Brothers, 1911.

Thompson, J. *Organizations in Action.* New York: McGraw-Hill, 1967.

Treiman, D.J., and Hartman, H.O., (eds.) *Women, Work and Wages: Equal Pay for Jobs of Equal Value.* Washington, DC: National Academy Press, 1981.

Velasquez, M.G. *Business Ethics: Cases and Concepts.* Englewood Cliffs, NJ: Prentice Hall, 1999.

Vroom, V. *Work and Motivation.* New York: John Wiley and Sons, 1964.

Weber, M. *The Protestant Ethic and the Spirit of Capitalism.* London: George Allen and Unwin, 1930.

Weisbord, M.R. *Organizational Diagnosis: A Workbook of Theory and Practice.* Reading, MA: Addison-Wesley Publishing Co., 1978.

Weiss, R. *The American Myth of Success.* New York: Basic Books, 1969.

Williams, R.W. *American Society: A Sociological Interpretation* (3rd ed.). New York: Alfred A. Knopf, 1970.

Wooden, J., and Jamison, S. *Wooden: A Lifetime of Observations and Reflections On and Off the Court.* Chicago: NTC/Contemporary Publishing Group, 1997.

Zager, R., and Rosow, M.P. (eds.) *The Innovative Organization: Productivity Programs in Action.* Elmsford, NY: Pergamon Press, 1982.

Zeleny, R.O. (ed.) *The World Book Encyclopedia* (20 vols.) Chicago: Field Enterprises Educational Corporation, 1965.

Articles
★★★

Adams, J.S. "Toward an Understanding of Inequity." *Journal of Abnormal and Social Psychology,* 1963, 67, 422-436.

Adams, J.S. "Inequity in Social Exchange," in Berkowitz, L. (ed.) *Advances in Experimental Social Psychology* (vol 2). New York: Academic Press, 1965.

Bergman, T.J., and Hills, F.S. "Internal Labor Markets and Indirect Pay Discrimination." *Compensation Review,* 1982, 14 (4), 41-50.

Bem, D.J. "Self-Perception: An Alternative Interpretation of Cognitive Dissonance Phenomena." *Psychological Review,* 1967, 74, 183-200.

Bloom, D.E., and Killingsworth, M.R. "Pay Discrimination in Research and Litigation: The Use of Regression." *Industrial Relations,* 1982, 21 (3), 318-339.

Boulding, K. "General Systems Theory: The Skeleton of Science." *Management Science,* 1956, 2 (3), 197-208.

Clarkson, M.B.E. "A Stakeholder Framework for Analyzing and Evaluating Corporate Social Performance." *Academy of Management Review*, 1995, 20, 92-117.

Collett, M.J. "Comparable Worth: An Overview." *Public Personnel Management*, 1983, 12 (4), 325-331.

Cook, A.H. "Comparable Worth: Recent Developments in Selected States." *Labor Law Journal*, 1983, 34 (8), 494-504.

Cranston, A. "The Proposed Equity Act of 1985." *Labor Law Journal*, 1985, 36 (3), 131-144.

Davis, L.E., and Taylor, J.C. "Technology, Organization and Job Structure," in Dubin, R. (ed.) *Handbook of Work, Organization and Society*. Chicago: Rand-McNally, 1976.

Deutsch, S. "Extending Workplace Democracy: Struggles to Come in Job Safety and Health." *Labor Studies Journal*, 1981, 6, 124-132.

Emery, F., and Trist, E. "The Causal Texture of Organizational Environments." *Human Relations*, 1965, 18, 21-32.

Festinger, L.A. "A Theory of Social Comparison Processes." *Human Relations*, May 1954, 117-140.

Forstmann, T. "Capitalism Promotes Positive Values," in Hurley, J.A. *American Values: Opposing Viewpoints*. San Diego: Greenhaven Press, 2000.

Fox, W. M. "Purpose and Validity in Job Evaluation." *Personnel Journal*, October, 1962, 432-437.

Gardner, S.E., and Daniel, C. "Implementing Comparable Worth/Pay Equity: Experiences of Cutting-Edge States." *Public Personnel Management*, 1998, 27 (4), 475-489.

Golper, J.B. "The Current Legal Status of Comparable Worth in the Federal Courts." *Labor Law Journal*, 1983, 34 (9), 563-580.

Gouldner, A.W. "The Norm of Reciprocity: A Preliminary Statement." *American Sociological Review*, 1960, 25, 161-179.

Grune, J.A., and Reder, N. "Pay Equity: An Innovative Public Policy Approach to Eliminating Sex-Based Wage Discrimination." *Public Personnel Management*, 1983, 12 (4), 395-403.

Hackman, J.R., and Oldham, G.R. "Motivation Through the Design of Work: Test of a Theory." *Organizational Behavior and Human Performance*, 1976, 16, 250-279.

Hallock, M. "Pay Equity: Did it Work?," in King, M.C. (ed.) *Squaring Up: Policy Strategies to Raise Women's Incomes in the United States.* Ann Arbor, MI: University of Michigan Press, 2001.

Hamner, W.C., and Harnett, D.L. "Goal-Setting Performance, and Satisfaction in an Interdependent Task." *Organizational Behavior and Human Performance*, 1974, 12, 217-230.

Harrison, R.V. "Person-Environment Fit and Job Stress," in Cooper, C.L. and Payne, R. (eds.) *Stress At Work.* New York: John Wiley and Sons, 1978.

Hartman, H.O., and Treiman, D.J. "Notes on the NAS Study of Equal Pay for Jobs of Equal Value." *Public Personnel Management*, 1983, 12 (4), 395-403.

Hildebrand, G. "The Market System," in Livernash, E.R. (ed.) *Comparable Worth: Issues and Alternatives* (2nd ed.). Washington D.C.: Equal Employment Advisory Council, 1984, 79-106.

Homans, G.C. "Social Behavior as Exchange." *American Journal of Sociology*, 1958, 63, 597-606.

House, R.J. "A Path-Goal Theory of Leadership." *Administrative Science Quarterly*, 1971, 16, 321-338.

Johannesson, R.E., Pierson, D.A., and Koziara, K.S. "Comparable Worth: The Measurement Dilemma." *Proceedings of the Thirty-Fifth Annual Meeting, Industrial Relations Research Association*, December 28-30, 1982, 162-168.

Kaplan, R.S., and Norton, D.P. "The Balanced Scorecard: Measures that Drive Performance." *Harvard Business Review*, January-February, 1992, 71-80.

Katz, D. "The Motivational Basis of Organizational Behavior." *Behavioral Science*, 1964, 9, 131-146.

Kerr, C., and Fisher, L.H. "Effects of Environment and Administration on Job Evaluation." *Harvard Business Review*, May, 1950, 77-96.

Klimoski, R.J., and Hayes, N.J. "Leader Behavior and Subordinate Motivation." *Personnel Psychology*, 1980, 33 (3), 543-555.

Lawler, E.E., and O'Gara, P.W. "Effects of Inequity Produced by Underpayment on Work Output, Work Quality, and Attitudes Toward the Work." *Journal of Applied Psychology*, 1967, 51, 403-410.

Lindahl, L. "What Makes a Good Job." *Personnel*, January 1949, 25.

Locke, E.A. "Toward a Theory of Task Motivation and Incentives." *Organizational Behavior and Human Performance*, 1968, 3, 157-189.

Lockerman, D. "Robert W. Woodruff: 50 Years at the Top." *Atlanta Magazine*, April 1973.

Maslow, A.H. "Theory Z." *Journal of Transpersonal Psychology*, 1969, 1 (2), 31-47.

McConomy, S., and Ganschinietz, B. "Trends in Job Evaluation Practices of State Personnel Systems: 1981 Survey Findings." *Public Personnel Management*, 1983, 12 (1), 1-12.

Meyer, H. "The Pay for Performance Dilemma." *Organizational Dynamics*, Winter 1975, 39-50.

Mezirow, J. "A Critical Theory of Adult Learning and Education." *Adult Education*, 1981, 32 (1), 3-27.

Milkovich, G.T., and Broderick, R. "Pay Discrimination: Legal Issues and Implications for Research." *Industrial Relations*, 1982, 21 (3), 309-317.

Mowday, R.T. "Equity Theory Predictions of Behavior in Organizations," in Steers, R.M., and Porter, L.W. *Motivation and Work Behavior* (3rd ed.). New York: McGraw-Hill, 1983.

Paine, L.S. "Managing for Organizational Integrity." *Harvard Business Review*, March/April 1994, 106-117.

Peters, E., and Extercatte, C. (eds.) "KPMG International Survey of Corporate Responsibility Reporting." Amsterdam: University of Amsterdam and KPMG Global Sustainability Services, 2005.

Pinder, C.C. "Concerning the Application of Human Motivation Theories in Organizational Settings." *Academy of Management Review*, July 1972, 384-397.

Pinder, C.C. "Additivity vs. Nonadditivity of Intrinsic and Extrinsic Incentives." *Journal of Applied Psychology*, 1977, 61 (6), 693-700.

Post, J.E. "Global Corporate Citizenship: Principles to Live and Work By." *Business Ethics Quarterly*, 2002, 12 (2), 143-153.

Pritchard, R.D. "Equity Theory: A Review and Critique." *Organizational Behavior and Human Performance*, 1969, 4, 176-211.

Pritchard, R.D., Dunnette, M.D., and Jorgenson, D.O. "Effects of Perceptions of Equity and Inequity on Worker Performance and Satisfaction." *Journal of Applied Psychology*, 1972, 56, 75-94.

Randstad Holding nv. "2006 Employee Review." Atlanta: Randstad North America, LP, 2006.

Remick, H. "The Comparable Worth Controversey." *Public Personnel Management*, 1981, 10 (4), 371-383.

Salancik, G.R. "Interaction Effects of Performance and Money on Self-Perception of Intrinsic Motivation." *Organizational Behavior and Human Performance*, June 1975, 339-351.

Sarbin, T.R., and Allen, V.L. "Role Theory," in Lindzey, G., and Aronson, E. (eds.) *The Handbook of Social Psychology* (vol 1, 2nd ed.). Reading, MA: Addison-Wesley, 1968.

Schachter, S., and Singer, J. "Cognitive, Social, and Physiological Determinants of Emotional State." *Psychological Review*, 1962, 69, 379-399.

Schuler, R.S. "The Effects of Role Perceptions on Employee Satisfaction and Performance Moderated by Employee Ability." *Organizational Behavior and Human Performance*, 1977, 18, 98-107.

Simon, H. "Theories of Decision Making in Economics and Behavioral Science." *American Economic Review*, 1959, 49 (3), 253-280.

Sklar, H., and Sherry, Rev. P.H. "A Just Minimum Wage: Good for Workers, Business and our Future." Washington, D.C.: American Friends Service Committee and The National Council of Churches USA, 2005.

Smith, L. "The President's Perspective." *Refresher USA*, 1975, 7 (3), 6-7.

Thompson, D.E., and Thompson, T.A. "Court Standards for Job Analysis in Test Validation." *Personnel Psychology*, 1982, 35 (4), 865-874.

Treiman, D.J. "Job Evaluation: An Analytical Review." Interim Report to the Equal Employment Opportunity Commission. Washington, D.C.: National Academy of Sciences, 1979.

U.S. Census Bureau and the Bureau of Labor and Statistics. "Annual Demographic Survey." Washington, DC, March 2005.

U.S. General Accounting Office. "Women's Earnings: Work Patterns Partially Explain Difference Between Men's and Women's Earnings." Washington, DC: Report GAO-04-35, 2003.

Vanous, J.P. "The Role of Individual Differences in Human Reactions to Job Characteristics." *Journal of Applied Psychology*, 1974, 59 (5), 616-622.

Walster, E., Berscheid, E., and Waister, W. "New Directions in Equity Research." *Journal of Personality and Social Psychology*, 1973, 25, 151-176.

Watts, P., and Holme, L. "Corporate Social Responsibility: Meeting Changing Expectations." Geneva: WBCSD Publications, 1999.

Weick, K.E. "The Concept of Equity in the Perception of Pay." *Administrative Science Quarterly*, 1967, 2, 414-439.

Weick, K.E. "Educational Organizations as Loosely Coupled Systems." *Administrative Science Quarterly*, 1976, 12 (1), 1-11.

Weick, K.E., and Nesset, B. "Preferences Among Forms of Equity." *Organizational Behavior and Human Performance*, November 1968, 3, 400-416.

Weiner, N. "Determinants and Behavioral Consequences of Pay Satisfaction: A Comparison of Two Models." *Personnel Psychology*, 1980, 33, 741-757.

Wicks, A.C. "The Value Dynamics of Total Quality Management: Ethics and the Foundations of TQM." *Business Ethics Quarterly*, 2001, 11 (3), 501-536.

Zuckerman, M. "Development of a Sensation-Seeking Scale." *Journal of Consulting Psychology*, 1964, 28, 477-482.

Court Cases Relating to Pay Equity
★★★

Briggs v. City of Madison, 536 F. Supp. 435 (W.D. Wisc. 1982).

County of Washington v. Gunther, 452 U.S. 161 (1981).

Lemons v. City and County of Denver, 17 FEP Cases 906 (D. Col. 1978), aff'd 620 F. 2d 228, 22 FEP Cases 959 (10th Cir. 1980).

Taylor v. Charley Bros. Co., 25 FEP Cases 602 (W.D. Pa. 1981).

Wilkins v. Univ. of Houston, 654 F. 2d 388 (5th Cir. 1981), vacated and remained, 103 S. Ct. 34 (1982), aff'd on remand, 695 F. 2d 134 (5th Cir. 1983).

The family has always been the cornerstone of American society. Our families nurture, preserve, and pass on to each succeeding generation the values we share and cherish, values that are the foundation of our freedoms.

Ronald Reagan

Printed in the United States
63019LVS00002B/400-450

9 780976 586814